NEW ERA OF OCEAN POLITICS

Studies in International Affairs Number 22

Y0-ABH-099

Studies in International Affairs Number 22

NEW ERA OF OCEAN POLITICS

by Ann L. Hollick and Robert E. Osgood

The Washington Center of Foreign Policy Research
School of Advanced International Studies
The Johns Hopkins University

The Johns Hopkins University Press
Baltimore and London

Copyright © 1974 by The Johns Hopkins University Press
All rights reserved. No part of this book may be reproduced
or transmitted in any form or by any means, electronic or
mechanical, including photocopying, recording, xerography, or
any information storage and retrieval system, without permission
in writing from the publisher. Manufactured in the United States
of America.

The Johns Hopkins University Press, Baltimore, Md. 21218
The Johns Hopkins University Press Ltd., London

Library of Congress Catalog Card Number 74–6833

ISBN 0–8018–1633–5 (clothbound edition)
ISBN 0–8018–1634–3 (paperbound edition)

Originally published, 1974
Paperbound edition, 1974

Library of Congress Cataloging in Publication data
will be found on the last printed page of this book.

CONTENTS

FOREWORD

Since 1967 the United States government has been actively engaged in formulating policy for the control and use of the oceans. Among the areas of international and "transnational" relations which are qualitatively new and important, regulation of the world's ocean space—subsoil of the seabed, water column, and air above—is in the forefront. It remains to be seen whether ocean policies will become as central to world politics as they once were, but already they have proved to be more pervasive and complicated in their effects on a great many nations. Involving a network of issues—the exploitation of the seabed, the breadth of the territorial sea, transit rights through straits, and the conservation and allocation of fishery resources—few areas of foreign policy encompass such a complex array of legal, political, military, economic, commercial, scientific, and ecological concerns in the United States and abroad. Indeed, few policy areas involve so complex an interaction of domestic and foreign policy interests and orientations within the U.S. government.

At the heart of these ocean issues (and of the debate on the law of the sea proposed to cope with them) is the allocation and use of ocean space. In the broadest sense, the main contention is between coastal economic interests and global maritime interests. Beyond this division of interests, however, simple categories fail to explain the constantly shifting political relationships in the law of the sea negotiations. In these, as in other international negotiations, the participants include governments, international organizations, and private interests. Each of these participants may support either a coastal or a maritime policy or a combination of the two.

The factors determining adoption of a coastal or maritime policy or a combination are diverse—a country's military position and needs, its level of economic development, whether a country has a broad or narrow continental shelf, whether it has a long or short coast or none at all, whether it lies athwart a significant international strait or has valuable offshore resources (living or nonliving), whether a national or private participant is primarily a producer or importer, a seller or consumer, a user or a supplier of ocean resources and space. The combinations (or transnational linkages) that may result are as diverse as the nations and interests involved. The U.S. or Canadian environmentalist who wishes to protect the national shoreline from marine pollution, urges extended offshore jurisdiction—much as the petroleum industry, but for different reasons. The uncomfortably allied petroleum and environmental interest groups find much in common with those Latin American governments seeking international recognition of their claims to 200-mile territorial waters. Internationalists seeking to maximize the extent of the "common heritage of mankind" side with naval and defense interests of the major maritime states who are anxious to curb coastal state assertions of jurisdiction. These alliances shift with the issue at hand—as when the petroleum industry, once it has secured offshore oil, turns to problems of transporting petroleum across the oceans and joins the naval interests in opposition to a variety of coastal state antipollution and navigational safety zones.

Alliances between governments are equally important to ocean policy. While Kenya, Sri Lanka, and Canada may support common fisheries proposals but pursue different approaches to the deep seabed regime, the major maritime powers are divided on fisheries matters but united on the need for guaranteed transit through international straits. Developing coastal states seek maximum control of offshore resources, but many land-locked and shelf-locked nations, regardless of their level of development—since they have nothing to gain from coastal state extensions of jurisdiction—support proposals of maritime states to restrict national jurisdiction and extend international control and revenue sharing. Alignments and oppositions formed on the basis of commercial and resource interests, however, are modified by regional affiliation, differences between developed and developing nations in the United Nations, and other affinities and distinctions.

After 1967, the forum for international negotiations between these allied and contending forces was the United Nations Seabed Committee.[1] In December, 1973, the Third United Nations Conference on the Law of the Sea opened in New York with more than 145 states participating. This two-week organizing session covered questions such as membership, allocation of committee seats, and voting procedures for the conference. Due to the disagreement of delegations on the rules of procedure, the voting question was carried into the first substantive session of

---

[1] Established as an ad hoc committee, and then a permanent one, the Committee on the Peaceful Uses of the Seabed and the Ocean Floor Beyond the Limits of National Jurisdiction was officially designated as the preparatory body for the Third United Nations Conference on the Law of the Sea in 1970. G.A. Res. 2750 (1970), 10 International Legal Materials 224 (1971).

the conference, held in the summer of 1974 in Caracas, Venezuela. The agenda items for the conference included international control of the seabed, the breadth of the territorial sea, the nature and extent of a coastal state economic zone beyond the territorial sea, straits used for international navigation, preservation of the marine environment, and scientific research. Given the great number of nations participating, the diversity of their interests, and the length of the agenda, plans were made for continuing the conference in a 1975 session in Vienna, Austria. The accomplishments of these conferences, in terms of reaching agreed principles and rules for the use of the oceans, will mark only the beginning of a long period of conflict and accommodation, of strife, and of the pursuit of order in ocean politics.

The complexity and rapid pace of negotiations and preparations for negotiations on the law of the sea treaty, together with the constantly changing national ocean policies, preclude any definitive assessment of the state of the new ocean politics.

In a series of papers and colloquia, of which this book is a part, the Ocean Policy Project at the Johns Hopkins University School of Advanced International Studies seeks to analyze some of the more enduring aspects of this subject and relate them to developing U.S. ocean policy.[2] Hollick's piece—an extension of articles that she has published in professional and popular journals—explains the basic issues, the configuration of national and transnational interests, and the processes of international

[2] The Project has been supported primarily by a grant from the National Science Foundation, which, however, bears no responsibility for the views expressed in this book.

negotiations and national policymaking that underlie the new ocean politics. These elements are then related to U.S. ocean policy and policymaking. Osgood examines a central concern of U.S. ocean policy: the relation of the prospective law of the sea treaty to U.S. security interests in the control and use of the oceans. Together, these pieces are a partial introduction to the early phase of an era of ocean history that will surely outlast most of the contemporary issues. Yet the future of ocean politics may be determined by the way these issues are resolved or left unresolved in the next few years.

ROBERT E. OSGOOD

I. BUREAUCRATS AT SEA

ANN L. HOLLICK

Assistant Professor, American Foreign Policy
School of Advanced International Studies
The Johns Hopkins University

Executive Director, U.S. Ocean Policy Project

The United States is among the world's foremost maritime powers. Given its two long coastlines and its Hawaiian, Micronesian, and Alaskan archipelagos, it is also a nation with substantial coastal interests.[1] The ocean policy decision-making process in the United States government is therefore fraught with conflict between coastal and maritime interests; the policy product therefore represents a series of tenuous compromises. Since the first announcements in 1970 of U.S. policies on seabed resource exploitation and other law of the sea issues, policy compromises have evolved steadily away from positions favoring military-strategic interests to positions more congenial to coastal and economic interests. This evolution has been due in part to international pressures and in part to the increased policy influence of domestic interest groups with economic and coastal concerns. The ability of coastal and economic interests to effect these changes has been enhanced by the emergence of international centers of economic and strategic power and the concommitant emphasis on national economic power and competition for resources.

[1] Indeed under a universal 200-mile territorial sea, the United States would gain more territory than any other nation. U.S., Department of State, Office of the Geographer, *Limits in the Seas*, no. 46, August 12, 1972, p. 5.

1

Developments in U.S. ocean policy fall roughly into two broad phases coinciding with the Nixon administration's first and second terms. The years 1968 through 1972 were characterized by the growth of a policy dispute between coastal and maritime interests within the government, White House resolution of that dispute in favor of strategic interests in May, 1970, and then a gradual return to parity between resource and strategic interests. In 1973 and 1974 the warfare between global strategic and coastal economic interests was subtly transformed into a conflict between political strategic and resource-oriented economic perspectives. By 1973 the issue of the extent of coastal state jurisdiction had been more or less decided by international sentiment in favor of broad zones of resource control, and U.S. strategic interests retreated to a strong defense of freedom of transit through and over international straits. The single area where policy latitude remained—the deep seabed regime—replaced the coastal areas as the focus of intragovernmental and international contention. This central conflict was blurred and diffused by the vast number of issues under consideration (ranging from prevention of marine pollution to compulsory settlement of disputes) and the need to accommodate them in a single United States policy on law of the sea. Additional factors distinguishing the pre- and post-1972 periods are the participation of a larger number of governmental agencies and bureaucratic actors and the active involvement of higher levels of government on a more frequent basis.

As announced in August, 1970, United States policy on exploitation of seabed minerals favored a narrow zone of national jurisdiction and the establishment of an international seabed regime beyond.[2] Exclusive coastal state control over the mineral resources of the continental shelf would extend only to the depth of 200 meters. Beyond that, in an intermediate zone reaching to the outer edge of the continental margin, the coastal state would act as a "trustee" for the international seabed authority. The international machinery would license the exploitation of minerals and a substantial portion of the revenues generated in the international area, including the "trusteeship zone," would be distributed among developing nations.

Since the announcement of this policy over four years ago, there has been a shift in U.S. policy away from insistence that national jurisdiction over seabed mineral resources be limited to the 200-meter isobath to acceptance of a 200-mile economic zone. By 1972 it had become apparent that the United States was willing to accommodate the strong international and domestic pressures favoring a 200-mile coastal state resource or economic zone. Policy statements after 1972 stressed the international standards that should apply in a seabed resource zone and have noted strong international support for broad coastal resource zones. In the coastal seabed economic area, the United States urged international agreement to sharing revenues, international standards regarding protection of the marine environment, noninterference with other uses of the area, integrity of investments and compulsory settlement of disputes. These principles were incorporated into

[2] United Nations, General Assembly, *Draft United Nations Convention on the International Seabed Area,* UN Doc. A/AC. 138/25 (1970).

draft treaty language and presented to the UN Seabed Committee in July, 1973. When the United
States presented its draft articles on a 200-mile
economic zone at the Caracas session of the Law of
the Sea Conference, the same principles were spelled
out in treaty language.[3]

On the second set of major policy issues before
the United States government, there has been a similar movement toward accommodating coastal interests after 1972. The American position on the
breadth of the territorial sea, international straits,
and fisheries, was first announced in 1970 and officially presented to the UN Seabed Committee in
July, 1971.[4] The government indicated that it was
prepared to agree to a 12-mile territorial sea provided that international agreement was reached on
freedom of transit through and over international
straits that would be overlapped by territorial seas.
The third provision in this set of proposals granted
limited preferential rights to the coastal state over
fishery resources off its shores. The U.S. position
on a 12-mile territorial sea and freedom of transit
through international straits has not changed substantially from the 1971 draft articles. Despite the
general acceptance of 12-mile territorial seas and
despite intense domestic and international pressures
in 1972 to settle for something less than freedom of
transit in international straits, U.S. strategic inter-

[3] United Nations, Third Conference on the Law of the Sea,
United States of America: Draft Articles for a Chapter on the
Economic Zone and the Continental Shelf, UN Doc. A/CONF.
62/C.2/L.47 (August 8, 1974).

[4] United Nations, General Assembly, *Draft Articles on the
Breadth of the Territorial Sea, Straits and Fisheries Submitted
by the United States of America,* UN Doc. A/AC.138/SC.II/
L.4 (July 30, 1971).

ests have stood fast on this policy. U.S. fishery policy, however, has evolved toward coastal state management of fisheries within the 200-mile zone. In 1972, the U.S. submitted new draft articles on fisheries,[5] this time not attached to the issues of territorial seas and straits. In addition to preferential rights, these articles provided for coastal state regulation of coastal and anadromous [6] species. This policy was superseded in 1974 by the U.S. draft articles on a 200-mile economic zone granting the coastal state "exclusive rights for the purpose of regulating fishing within the economic zone" and including special provisions for anadromous and highly migratory species.

The United States proposed treaty articles in 1973 on a third set of issues—marine pollution, scientific research and technical assistance, and compulsory settlement of disputes. Articles on the marine environment reflected an effort to satisfy the domestic and international coastal viewpoint without seriously hampering international navigation.[7] They proposed international standards for seabed-source and vessel-source pollution. While the coastal state would have the right to set stricter standards and the power of enforcement in the event of pollution resulting from seabed exploitation, its standard-setting and enforcement powers would be limited in the area of vessel-source pollution. The interna-

[5] United Nations, General Assembly, *United States Revised Draft Fisheries Article,* UN Doc. A/AC.138/SC.II/L.9 (August 4, 1972).

[6] Spawning in fresh water, as salmon.

[7] United Nations, General Assembly, *United States Draft Articles on the Protection of the Marine Environment and the Prevention of Marine Pollution,* UN Doc. A/AC.138/SC.III/L.40 (July 18, 1973).

tional standards adopted by the Intergovernmental Maritime Consultative Organization (IMCO) would be primarily enforced by flag and port states with coastal state enforcement in cases of imminent harmful damage.

Where a domestic coastal input has been absent, as in the formulation of marine science policy, the U.S. treaty proposal nonetheless reflects an effort to accommodate the sentiments of coastal states in the hope of avoiding future coastal state restrictions on scientific research. U.S. draft articles on scientific research [8] stress the benefits of marine science and the obligation of the marine scientist to ensure that those benefits are enjoyed by the coastal state. In the area beyond the territorial sea, the obligations include advance notification, coastal state right of participation in research, sharing of data and samples, open publication of research results, assistance to the coastal state in assessing the implications of the research results and compliance with international environmental standards.

The U.S. submission of a set of draft articles [9] on compulsory settlement of disputes in the oceans is premised on the view that the substantive articles of any law of the sea treaty to be agreed will not suffice to avoid conflict regarding the use of ocean space. The means to settle these disputes would include general, regional or special agreement but where states have not agreed to such procedures, a

[8] United Nations, General Assembly, *United States of America: Draft Articles for a Chapter on Marine Scientific Research,* UN Doc. A/AC.138/SC.III/L.44 (July 20, 1973).

[9] United Nations, General Assembly, *United States of America: Draft Articles for a Chapter on the Settlement of Disputes,* UN Doc. A/AC.138/97 (August 22, 1973).

law of the sea tribunal would be available and its decisions would be binding.

One cannot understand the U.S. position on these ocean issues without understanding the pressures and concessions produced by diverse national and commercial interests as they interact with these same kinds of interests in other countries. These pressures and concessions are transmitted through a policy process that ultimately shapes the U.S. position. Although the process of formulating ocean policy is in many ways distinctive, it nonetheless illuminates some perennial features of the foreign policy decision-making process, with particular reference in this case to the Nixon administration and the operation of its National Security Council.

Perhaps the most fruitful approach to understanding the formulation of ocean policy is that of bureaucratic politics. In this approach the actors or "makers" of ocean policy are public officials and large bureaucracies engaged in a continuous process of bargaining which is influenced throughout by domestic as well as foreign interests. The ocean policies that result are a product of contention—within the government and with domestic and foreign interests —and not of a rational centralized decision-making process.[10]

Several low-level generalizations or lessons emerge from a bureaucratic politics approach to

[10] The bureaucratic politics approach to foreign policy is most articulately elaborated in Graham T. Allison, "Conceptual Models and the Cuban Missile Crisis," *American Political Science Review,* LXIII, no. 3 (September, 1969), pp. 689–718; Morton H. Halperin, "Why Bureaucrats Play Games," *Foreign Policy* (Spring 1971); Graham T. Allison and Morton H. Halperin, "Bureaucratic Politics: A Paradigm and Some Policy Implications," *World Politics,* XXIV, Supplement, Spring 1972, pp. 40–79.

ocean policy. First, it is apparent that the ocean policy process involves a blend of domestic and foreign policy considerations. As domestic interests have become more involved in the process, the foreign policy latitude of both the State Department and White House has diminished correspondingly. While decisions and policies on the oceans have remained a product of conflict and compromise, the active participation of domestic interests has restricted the process of tradeoffs. Bureaucrats who initially interjected themselves into the range of ocean issues now concentrate on those issues of direct relevance to their agency.

The policy process has been characterized by contention between interests with varying degrees of political and economic power. The most powerful private interest in the seabed debate has been the petroleum industry. Equally powerful and initially in opposition to the petroleum position is the Defense Department, representing more traditional foreign policy considerations regarding use of the oceans. A recent entrant into the ocean policy game, and one with significant power, is the Treasury Department under George Shultz and later William Simon. What emerges from an examination of the policy role of these and other ocean interest groups is the not too surprising fact that an interest's influence on policy is a function of its position within the government, of its economic and political power,[11] of its access to contacts within the bureaucracy, the Congress and the White House, of its ability to glean information, and of the skill of its policy partisans.

[11] Tables 1 and 2 provide a rough index of priorities accorded to agencies and ocean uses by the federal government.

TABLE 1

Total Federal Marine Science Program and Percent of Total by Major Purpose: FYs 1966–1974 [a]

Major Purpose	1966		1967		1968		Estimated 1969		Estimated 1970		Estimated 1971		Estimated 1972		Estimated 1973		Estimated 1974	
	$	%	$	%	$	%	$	%	$	%	$	%	$	%	$	%	$	%
National security	125.4	37.6	161.8	36.9	119.9	27.8	127.2	27.4	127.0	24.7	102.0	19.6	92.1	14.7	92.9	14.9	102.4	15.9
Oceanographic research	71.6	21.5	61.5	14.0	78.1	18.1	78.4	16.9	78.4	15.2	101.5	19.4	119.4	19.1	109.9	17.7	116.1	18.1
Ocean exploration, mapping, charting and geodesy	32.3	9.7	77.4	17.7	75.7	17.5	79.7	17.2	89.9	17.5	79.7	15.1	85.2	13.6	86.0	13.8	89.3	13.9
Fishery development and seafood technology	38.7	11.6	38.1	8.7	40.1	9.3	45.3	9.8	49.8	9.7	45.5	8.7						
Living resources													76.4	12.2	80.5	12.9	82.1	12.8
Development and conservation of the coastal zone	19.9	6.0	21.4	4.9	27.6	6.4	32.1	6.9	43.5	8.5	48.9	9.4	94.2	15.0	91.2	14.7	88.8	13.8
Environmental observation and prediction	13.7	4.1	24.4	5.6	28.8	6.7	33.7	7.3	39.8	7.7	43.0	8.2	34.7	5.6	31.9	5.1	37.8	5.9
Transportation	10.4	3.1	11.9	2.7	11.1	2.6	16.7	3.6	23.5	4.5	37.3	7.1	35.8	5.7	39.0	6.3	39.1	6.1
General purpose ocean engineering	3.5	1.0	14.8	3.4	19.2	4.4	19.1	4.1	24.8	4.8	29.1	5.6	35.9	5.7	33.2	5.3	34.3	5.3

	$	%	$	%	$	%	$	%	$	%	$	%	$	%	$	%	$	%
International cooperation and collaboration	5.1	1.5	7.1	1.5	9.6	2.2	8.4	1.8	10.0	1.9	8.8	1.7	9.5	1.5	10.0	1.6	10.5	1.7
Health	5.1	1.5	6.6	1.5	5.3	1.2	6.0	1.4	5.4	1.0	5.9	1.1	17.4	2.8	19.7	3.2	22.3	3.5
Nonliving resources	3.8	1.1	7.2	1.6	7.3	1.7	8.0	1.7	10.5	2.4	11.4	2.2	8.9	1.4	8.2	1.3	8.2	1.3
Education	2.2	0.7	4.0	0.9	7.0	1.6	6.7	1.4	8.2	1.6	6.9	1.3	16.7	2.7	19.8	3.2	10.9	1.7
National data centers	1.7	0.5	1.8	0.4	2.1	0.5	2.2	0.4	2.6	0.5	3.1	0.6						
Total	333.4	100.0	438.0	100.0	431.8	100.0	463.4	100.0	513.3	100.0	522.5	100.0	626.2	100.0	622.3	100.0	641.8	100.0

Note: All dollars are in millions, all percentages are of yearly totals.

[a] For FY data 1966–70 see the following publications by the U.S. National Council on Marine Resources and Engineering Development, Government Printing Office, Washington, D.C.

1966: *Marine Science Affairs—A Year of Transition*, February, 1967, p. 105.
1967: *Marine Science Affairs—A Year of Plans and Progress*, March, 1968, p. 171.
1968: *Marine Science Affairs—A Year of Broadened Participation*, January, 1969, p. 205.
1969: *Marine Science Affairs—Selecting Priority Programs*, April, 1970, p. 202.
1970: *Marine Science Affairs*, April, 1971, p. 13.

For FY 1971 see: U.S., Office of Science and Technology, *The Federal Ocean Program*, Government Printing Office, Washington, D.C., April, 1972, p. 106.

For FY 1972–74 see: U.S., Office of Science and Technology, *The Federal Ocean Program*, Government Printing Office, Washington, D.C., April, 1973, p. 84.

TABLE 2

Total Federal Marine Science Program by Department and Independent Agency: FYs 1966–1974 [a]

Agency	1966		1967		1968		Estimated 1969		Estimated 1970		Estimated 1971		Estimated 1972		Estimated 1973		Estimated 1974	
	$	%	$	%	$	%	$	%	$	%	$	%	$	%	$	%	$	%
Department of Defense	174.9	52.8	277.7	63.4	240.6	55.7	259.7	56.0	263.7	51.2	231.2	44.2	240.7	38.5	283.2	38.2	255.6	39.8
Department of Interior	56.5	15.2	64.1	14.6	70.5	16.3	80.8	17.4	29.2	5.6	27.5	5.3	39.7	6.3	40.3	6.5	43.7	6.8
National Science Foundation	47.7	14.4	24.8	5.7	38.1	8.6	34.9	7.5	30.3	6.4	49.4	9.5	65.7	10.5	57.3	9.2	61.1	9.5
Department of Commerce	25.0	7.5	35.3	8.0	33.6	7.8	38.1	8.2	118.3	23.1	139.3	26.7	163.8	26.1	168.0	27.0	170.9	26.6
Department of Transportation	8.1	2.4	8.3	1.9	15.4	3.6	19.8	4.3	23.4	4.5	34.3	6.6	62.8	10.0	59.1	9.5	49.6	7.7
Atomic Energy Commission	8.3	2.5	11.3	2.6	13.8	3.2	10.6	2.3	9.5	1.9	7.7	1.4	6.9	1.1	7.2	1.2	7.5	1.2
Department of Health, Education and Welfare	5.4	1.6	7.7	1.8	6.5	1.5	7.3	1.6	6.5	1.3	6.0	1.1	8.7	1.4	7.9	1.3	8.1	1.3
State Department	5.0	1.5	5.1	1.2	6.6	1.5	6.9	1.5	7.7	1.5	8.3	1.6	9.5[b]	1.5[b]	9.8[b]	1.6[b]	10.3[b]	1.6[b]
Smithsonian Institution	1.5	0.4	1.6	0.4	1.9	0.4	1.9	0.4	1.9	0.3	2.8	0.6	2.3	0.4	2.7	0.4	3.2	0.5
Agency for International Development	.1	[c]	2.0	0.5	3.0	0.7	1.5	0.3	2.3	0.4								

Agency	1966 $	%	1967 $	%	1968 $	%	1969 $	%	1970 $	%	1971 $	%	1972 $	%	1973 $	%	1974 $	%
National Aeronautics and Space Administration	.9	[c]	.1	[c]	1.8	0.4	1.9	0.4	2.3	0.4	3.3	0.7	4.2	0.7	7.4	1.2	7.1	1.1
Environmental Protection Agency									18.2	3.4	12.2	2.3	21.9	3.5	24.4	3.9	24.7	3.8
Total	333.4	100.0	438.0	100.0	431.8	100.0	463.4	100.0	513.3	100.0	522.0	100.0	626.2	100.0	622.3	100.0	641.8	99.9

Note: All dollars are in millions, all percentages are of yearly totals.

[a] For FY data 1966–70 see the following publications by the U.S. National Council on Marine Resources and Engineering Development, Government Printing Office, Washington, D.C.

1966: *Marine Science Affairs—A Year of Transition*, February, 1967, p. 109.
1967: *Marine Science Affairs—A Year of Plans and Progress*, March, 1968, p. 176.
1968: *Marine Science Affairs—A Year of Broadened Participation*, January, 1969, p. 211.
1969: *Marine Science Affairs—Selecting Priority Programs*, April, 1970, p. 201.
1970: *Marine Science Affairs*, April, 1971, p. 13.

For FY 1971 see: U.S., Office of Science and Technology, *The Federal Ocean Program*, Government Printing Office, Washington, D.C., April, 1972, p. 105.

For FY 1972–74 see: U.S., Office of Science and Technology, *The Federal Ocean Program*, Government Printing Office, Washington, D.C., April, 1973, p. 84.

[b] Includes Agency for International Development.
[c] Less than 0.1%.

Several observations can be made about the NSC system as it has operated with Henry Kissinger in the White House and then in the Department of State. During the first term of the Nixon administration, the NSC system funnelled all contentious ocean policy questions to the White House for resolution by Kissinger and perhaps the president. Where general agreement prevailed, lower level bureaucrats formulated policy. Where disagreement arose, the skillful bureaucrat was able to affect the outcome by judicious formulation and presentation of options for Presidential consideration. NSC staffers thus enjoyed an advantage over the Ehrlichman and Haldeman staffers in determining policy outcomes when a decision was to be taken in the NSC foreign policy channel.

With the departure of Ehrlichman and Haldeman from government and the creation of a system of government by "super-secretaries," the NSC system was altered. Compensating for the loss of a domestic affairs staff near the president was the expanded authority of Secretary of the Treasury George Shultz and the Director of the Office of Management and Budget Roy Ash. While these officials filled the economic policy vacuum left in the White House, the NSC mechanism continued to maintain jurisdiction over law of the sea. Kissinger's appointment as secretary of state, however, divided the NSC staff between the White House and the State Department and further diffused the NSC system's handling of issues, such as law of the sea, in which the new secretary had little interest. Further complicating the problem was the distance between Secretary Kissinger and the Deputy Secretary of State Kenneth Rush, who chaired the NSC Under Secretaries Committee. Shultz's departure from government and Rush's move to the White House as coordinator of economic policy did little to alter an already diffuse decision-making process.

In 1970, because White House officials and department secretaries either did not perceive ocean questions to be urgent or found the legal, political, economic, and strategic technicalities baffling, the ocean bureaucrats enjoyed substantial freedom from high-level supervision when concensus could be reached among the agencies or once the basic decisions were made. Due perhaps to the complexity of the subject, the U.S. ocean bureaucrats have tended to specialize in ocean issues and have been, for the most part, lawyers. The result until 1973 was a rather small group of ocean experts formulating policy isolated from other policy areas as well as from White House scrutiny.

In 1973 as new segments of the public were discovering the law of the sea, Secretary of the Treasury George Shultz and his deputy, William Simon, became actively concerned with the law of the sea. This interest was quickly transformed into alarm that the proposed U.S. policies might be such as to deter access to needed seabed resources in a time of increasing scarcity. A more fundamental source of concern was the recognition that decisions on ocean policy had been taken without thoroughgoing economic analyses.

The most obvious effect of the personal involvement of the secretary of the treasury on the policy process was to raise law of the sea policy to more prominent levels in other interested agencies. In 1970, the formulation of ocean policy had fallen back to lower levels of government after the Under

Secretaries Committee meeting and the presidential decision. Similarly in 1972, high-level interest waned after a White House decision on straits. After the 1973 meeting of the Under Secretaries Committee, however, a higher level of interest was sustained throughout the government. Whether this will abate remains to be seen. Among the imponderables are the changes President Ford may initiate as well as the extent to which Henry Kissinger can be interested in law of the sea in an era of detente, fighting in the Middle East and Cyprus, and the pressing problems of high level summitry. Even if ocean policy did capture his imagination, and depending upon the position he took, the outcome of a clash with the president's economic advisors at a time of intense concern with the economy is not a foregone conclusion. Becoming secretary of a department has made it increasingly difficult to maintain the third party arbiter role heretofore practiced by the National Security Council in agency disputes. The prospect of an accommodation between high-level officials would seem more likely than an effort to capture the attention of a new president.

UNITED STATES OCEAN POLICY

Seabed Policy: 1968–1970

Of the domestic interests affected by the disposition of the seabed and its mineral resources, only four had a significant influence on or involvement in policy formulation through 1972—the petroleum industry, the military, the hard minerals industry, and the marine science community. While the military and the marine scientist have developed a number of new ocean uses—such as locations for fixed detection devices, coring, and underwater habitats—their traditional and fundamental interest in the oceans has remained mobility and access. The petroleum and hard minerals industries, on the other hand, while concerned with commercial transport, are among the new users of the oceans with regard to the recovery of fixed seabed mineral resources. The resulting clash between the new and traditional ocean uses has been a central element in the formulation of U.S. seabed policy.

Seabed policy has two major aspects: (1) the delimitation of national jurisdiction over seabed minerals and (2) the nature of the seabed regime to be established beyond national jurisdiction. Each of the four interest groups has been concerned with different aspects of seabed policy. While the petroleum industry has been primarily concerned with the location of the boundary of national jurisdiction, the hard minerals industry is engaged in the seabed regime to be established beyond that boundary. The military and the marine scientist are affected by both of these questions insofar as they might restrict their mobility on the oceans. In 1969 and 1970 conflict first began over both the national boundary and the international regime issues— between the Defense Department and the petroleum industry in the former case and between the Defense Department and the hard minerals industry in the latter. The clash over the boundary question culminated earlier than that over the regime and was much more virulent, due in no small measure to the relative power parity of defense and petroleum interests. Only as general concensus developed by 1972 in favor of broad resource zones did the Department of Defense withdraw from active involvement in the boundary issue to concentrate on the straits question.

The policy dispute over the boundary originated in the 1968 discovery that seabed petroleum deposits are generally limited to the continental margin. Although offshore petroleum operations had been underway for over two decades, they were confined to the shallow areas of the continental shelf and knowledge of the area beyond was at best vague. In 1967 and early 1968, new discoveries and developments led the petroleum industry to reevaluate its interest in the deeper offshore areas. The proposal of Malta's ambassador, Arvid Pardo, at the United Nations [12] raised worldwide hopes of boundless seabed treasure while simultaneously threatening to jeopardize national access to them. In the same period, estimates of the magnitude of offshore petroleum resources were skyrocketing as technological advances were lowering the cost of deep water operations.

Important in unifying the entire petroleum industry around a single position on offshore jurisdiction were two reports emanating from the U.S. Geological Survey in early 1968. In the first, the director of the Geological Survey indicated that commercial petroleum deposits would be restricted to the continental margin and suggested that the legal definition of the continental shelf should be adapted

[12] United Nations, General Assembly, 22nd sess., *Declaration and Treaty Concerning the Reservation Exclusively for Peaceful Purposes of the Sea-Bed and of the Ocean Floor Underlying the Seas Beyond the Limits of Present National Jurisdiction, and the Use of their Resources in the Interests of Mankind,* A/6695 (August 18, 1967).

to correspond with the geological boundary.[13] The impact of this statement on subsequent petroleum policy was reinforced by new and substantially increased estimates of offshore petroleum resources. The Geological Survey reported recoverable reserves on the U.S. continental margins ranging from 180 to 220 billion barrels of petroleum liquids and from 820 to 1,100 trillion cubic feet of gas.[14]

On the basis of these findings, major segments of the U.S. petroleum industry moved quickly to stake out a policy position on the location of the continental shelf boundary. The National Petroleum Council offered a definitive policy formulation in its interim report entitled *Petroleum Resources Under the Ocean Floor*.[15] The NPC's argumentation combined an ingenious early version of a national "energy crisis" argument with elaborate geological and legal reasoning. Using the Interior Department's estimates, the NPC pointed to the substantial resources off U.S. shores and insisted that it was vital to the nation's security to guarantee national control of all the energy resources of the continental margin. The alternative, it was suggested, would

[13] U.S., Department of the Interior, Geological Survey, "Geologic Boundary of the Continents," statement of W. T. Pecora, February 21, 1968.

[14] U.S., Department of the Interior, V. E. McKelvey, et al., "Potential Mineral Resources of the United States Outer Continental Shelves," Unpublished Report of the Geological Survey to the Public Land Law Review Commission, March, 1968. A year later the Geological Survey estimated potential reserves in place to a depth of 200 meters to be 660–780 billion barrels of oil and 1,640–2,200 trillion cubic feet of natural gas with reserves of the same magnitude in the area between 200- and 2,500-meter isobaths.

[15] Published July, 1968; the final report came out in March, 1969.

be a dangerous dependence on foreign supplies of petroleum.

To secure national control of these offshore petroleum resources, the U.S. government was urged to unilaterally assert sovereign rights over offshore seabed resources to the outer edge of the continental margin. Such a move, the petroleum industry argued, would be consistent with the intent of the Geneva Convention on the Continental Shelf and would in no way impair high seas freedoms in the area. According to Article 1 of the 1958 Geneva Convention, coastal state jurisdiction over seabed resources, or the limit of the legal continental shelf, extends to the 200-meter (656 feet) isobath or beyond that to the depth that admits of exploitation. Although in 1969 producing wells were operating within the 200-meter isobath (at depths of 340 feet), exploratory wells were being drilled at depths far exceeding this limit (1,300 feet).[16] Adding the expected advance of recovery capabilities to the geological distinction between the margin and the deep seabed, the industry contended that the intent of the Geneva Convention was to advance the continental shelf boundary to the outer limit of the continental margin. Underlying this early petroleum position was the traditional belief shared by both the domestic and overseas branches of the petroleum industry that in gaining access to resources off the U.S. coasts as well as off those of other nations it was safer and more profitable for American firms to deal bilaterally with coastal nations than with an unfamiliar international regime possibly weighted

[16] U.S., Congress, Senate, Committee on Commerce, *Special Study on United Nations Suboceanic Lands Policy, Hearings,* 91st cong., 1st sess., 1969, p. 103.

against U.S. interests.[17] The 1970 and 1971 Teheran and Tripoli price agreements were still a year and a half in the future.

As the petroleum industry began to advance this position within the government, the Defense Department position on the boundary moved in the opposite direction. The military observed that the Interior Department's issuing of leases at depths far greater than the 200-meter isobath constituted de facto extension of the U.S. continental shelf based on the exploitability clause of the Geneva Convention. Although under the terms of the Continental Shelf Convention resource jurisdiction was not to affect other uses of the area, the military came increasingly to fear that such would not be the case. Not only was Defense concerned about the effect of such extensions on the placement of anti-submarine warfare detection devices, but it was equally fearful that the limited resource sovereignty delegated to a coastal state would gradually expand, through the phenomenon of "creeping jurisdiction," to claims of total territorial sovereignty. Thus the military came to the view that the seaward extension of the continental shelf boundary as exploitation proceeded, together with the expansion of coastal state sovereignty over superjacent waters, would ultimately close off U.S. naval access to coastal areas around the world.

[17] For articulate government statements of this view at the time see: U.S., Congress, Senate, Senator Hansen on the Seaward Limits of National Jurisdiction over the Continental Shelf, 91st cong., 2nd sess., April 16, 1970, *Congressional Record,* daily ed. pp. S5933 ff., and Congressman Bush on Treaty to Renounce All National Claims on Seabed Resources, 91st cong., 2nd sess., June 30, 1970, *Congressional Record,* daily ed., pp. H6272–73.

At that time the Defense Department solution to the threat of creeping jurisdiction was to attempt to limit the size of special purpose or resource zones in the oceans. Constrained from a resort to force to protect U.S. navigational rights from coastal state encroachment, Defense Department representatives opted for a broad international agreement through a formal conference. With regard to seabed minerals, the Defense Department sought international agreement on a continental shelf extending no farther than the 200-meter isobath. To sell such a scheme to governments of developing nations, Defense Department officials proposed the establishment of a generous and powerful seabed mineral regime in the area beyond the narrow continental shelf.[18] In an unsuccessful effort to convince the skeptical petroleum industry of the merits of such a boundary, Defense Department representatives pointed out that 92 percent of the world's continental margins were off foreign shores. To gain access to these, it was far better for the petroleum industry to deal with an impartial international seabed authority than to deal bilaterally with unpredictable national governments that might resort to harassment, profit squeezing or outright expropriation.[19] The technological superiority of the American petroleum industry and the dominant role that the U.S. government would probably play in an

[18] For statements of these points see Louis Henkin and Leigh Ratiner in Lewis M. Alexander, ed., *Law of the Sea: United Nations and Ocean Management* (Kingston, R.I.: Law of the Sea Institute, 1971), pp. 19, 325–27.

[19] Leigh S. Ratiner, "United States Oceans Policy," *Journal of Maritime Law and Commerce,* vol. 2, no. 2 (January, 1971), pp. 236–37.

international seabed authority would presumably assure favorable treatment of U.S. companies.

Inherent in the policy position that Defense was advancing within the government was a readiness to risk the petroleum industry's resource interests, as industry saw them, in return for internationally agreed rights of transit. The industry was predictably opposed to such a tradeoff and fought it vigorously through the Interior Department. The petroleum industry's ready access to information and to policy makers within the government contributed to its effective and early input into the policy-making process.

The hard minerals and marine science interests were less fortunate. Throughout 1969 and 1970 neither hard minerals nor science was adequately represented in the closely-held policy deliberations within the government. The hard minerals industry's concern in seabed policy has been with the nature of the regime rather than with the location of the continental shelf boundary. Of interest to the ocean miner is the manganese nodule—a dark, potato-shaped accretion containing varying amounts of a large number of minerals such as cobalt, nickel, copper, manganese, iron, silicon, and aluminum. While manganese nodules are scattered widely over the ocean floor, the nodules with the greatest proportion of commercially attractive cobalt, nickel, and copper are generally found in the deepest parts of the oceans (at depths as great as 18,000 feet).[20]

[20] David C. Brooks, "Deep Sea Manganese Nodules: From Scientific Phenomenon to World Resource," *Natural Resources Journal,* vol. 8 (July, 1968), pp. 406–7; Arnold J. Rothstein, "Deep Ocean Mining: Today and Tomorrow," *Columbia Journal of World Business,* vol. 6 (January-February, 1971), pp. 43–50.

Because nodules of commercial value are rarely found on the continental margin, locating the national continental shelf boundary at any point up to the outer edge of the margin will not significantly affect the miner of nodules.

First discovered in the 1870s, the manganese nodule came to be considered as a potential resource only recently. As information about nodules has increased, mining industry policy has undergone several transitions—from early support for a broad continental shelf, to a policy of a moving shelf boundary, to a total disregard of the boundary issue and a strong position on the regime beyond national jurisdiction. In August, 1968 the petroleum and hard minerals industries were in substantial agreement on the boundary question as was reflected in a joint report sent to the American Bar Association House of Delegates by the Sections of Natural Resources Law, International and Comparative Law, and the Standing Committee on Peace and Law Through the United Nations. The joint report supported the National Petroleum Council view that the rights of coastal states to the minerals of the seabed already extended to the foot of the continental margin. The report also deemed it premature to consider establishing a regime for the seabed beyond that boundary.

By 1969 the hard minerals interest group began to move away from this position. In the August, 1969 joint report by the same sections of the American Bar Association, the split was evident. The new joint report explicitly stated that some members no longer supported the interpretation of the continental shelf boundary that had been advocated a year before. Instead these members argued that the

Geneva Convention on the Continental Shelf "extends sovereign rights over the seabed beyond the 200-meter line only as technological progress makes exploitation in that area possible in fact." [21]

This newly independent position on the continental shelf boundary coincided with heightened industry interest in the recovery of manganese nodules and increased knowledge of the location of commercially attractive deposits. Although the mining industry shared the petroleum industry's aversion to international administrative organizations, it gradually came to the view that mining companies would be operating in areas beyond the limits of national jurisdiction no matter where the continental shelf boundary was drawn. Ocean miners became increasingly concerned, therefore, with the nature of the seabed regime which would govern deep sea exploitation—a concern which was not shared by the petroleum interest group at the time given petroleum's preoccupation with national seabed jurisdiction.

Despite the absence of a direct interest in the boundary issue, the hard minerals industry continued its involvement in the boundary dispute for tactical purposes through 1969 and 1970. The mining representatives were willing to support a narrow but outward moving boundary—if such a boundary could be used to buy a satisfactory seabed regime.[22] By

[21] American Bar Association, "Non-Living Resources of the Sea (A Critique), *Natural Resources Lawyer,* vol. 2 (November, 1969), p. 429.

[22] John G. Laylin, attorney at law, in U.S., Congress, Senate, Committee on Interior and Insular Affairs, *Outer Continental Shelf, Hearings,* Part I, 91st cong., 1st and 2nd sess., 1969 and 1970, p. 136.

. . . those who have primarily in mind the extraction of oil a "satisfactory regime," the hard minerals industry meant a system of freedom to explore the seabed, to stake claims and to receive exclusive licenses to exploit the claimed areas. An international authority, in this view, should be no more than a registry agency, and its financial exactions should be minimal.

Although the mining industry was willing to trade the petroleum industry's desired broad national shelf for a favorable seabed regime, it soon found the Defense Department to be a dangerous ally. To induce other nations to agree to a narrow limit on the continental shelf, Defense was urging the establishment of a powerful and generous seabed authority to administer the exploration and exploitation of seabed resources and to allocate substantial revenues from these activities to an international development fund. Despite its opposition to the Defense Department position, the hard minerals industry was not particularly successful in blocking it. Due to its position on the boundary, the hard minerals interest had lost the support of the petroleum industry. And within the Interior Department, hard minerals had to compete with petroleum for the

---

are interested only in the area landward of the foot of the continental slope. They have been informed, it would appear, that there is little likelihood of oil pools below the bed of the deep sea. In consequence they are not concerned with the regime to be established for the deep sea bed.

In contrast . . . [those] . . . who have in mind the interests of hard metal miners find themselves agreeing with many of the contentions of the Navy and the scientists. They do not object to a broad shelf, but they do object to sacrificing the chances of reaching agreement on a satisfactory deep sea regime by insisting willy nilly that the United States now take the position that the outer limit of the shelf is now at the foot of the continental slope.

time and energy of government bureaucrats responsible for seabed policy.

The problems of the marine science interest were somewhat different. Because the marine scientist shares the military's interest in unrestricted access to the world's oceans, he is concerned both with the continental shelf boundary and with the international regime beyond. However, the scientific community has taken the approach that it can and should distinguish its research in the oceans from commercial and military investigations. In all ocean policy efforts, therefore, the scientist has sought to include explicit guarantees for open scientific research. Such guarantees necessarily imply the absence of a similar freedom of military access for research, monitoring, and even transit. They have been resisted, therefore, by defense officials.

The policy position advocated by the United States in 1970, with its strong emphasis on maintaining ocean freedoms, was consonant with the overall needs of the scientific interest. While State Department officials representing marine science and, to a lesser extent, the National Science Foundation were in substantial agreement on the needs of marine research, they were unable to override military opposition to explicit guarantees for freedom of scientific research. The scientific community, therefore, failed to secure inclusion of its coveted guarantees for scientific freedom in the U.S. Draft Seabed Treaty of 1970.

An additional interest which has not been mentioned, and one with a limited influence on ocean policy until 1970, was that of the government's official foreign policy agency—the Department of

State. To date the State Department's guiding purpose has been to advance U.S. ocean interests in international negotiations while maintaining ordered and harmonious relations with other nations on a broad range of ocean issues. Its overriding bias has been toward reaching a widely accepted international law of the sea agreement. To achieve these objectives the Department of State has sought to maintain control over the formulation as well as the official presentation of U.S. ocean policies. This has evoked strenuous efforts to resolve domestic contention over ocean issues to arrive at a policy position acceptable to all parties. When the seabed issue was first introduced in the United Nations in 1967, the State Department encountered a series of obstacles to the achievement of its objectives. These impediments placed the State Department's UN officials in the unenviable position of apparent recalcitrance in the face of international pressures to address the seabed question. The first difficulty was that of resolving intra-State Department bureaucratic contention over control of ocean policy. This was settled in February, 1970 when the legal advisor, John R. Stevenson, became the head of a consolidated Law of the Sea Task Force,[23] a position which he held until his retirement from government in January, 1973.

The second difficulty plaguing the State Department's efforts to formulate seabed policy was the growing dispute between the Departments of In-

[23] A useful discussion of the role of the legal advisor within the Department of State may be found in Richard Bilder, "The Office of the Legal Advisor: The State Department Lawyer and Foreign Affairs," *American Journal of International Law,* vol. 56 (July, 1962), pp. 633–84.

terior and Defense. In a successful effort to forestall the imposition of a boundary policy by the State Department, the Department of Defense requested an Under Secretaries Committee review of the seabed boundary question. In response to this request, the White House issued a National Security Study Memorandum in April, 1969 [24] proposing that, in the absence of interagency agreement, the Under Secretaries Committee meet to consider the position that the United States should take at the United Nations regarding the location of the continental shelf boundary. The NSSM further proposed that the Under Secretaries Committee attempt to reconcile the U.S. position on the continental shelf boundary with that on the territorial sea and related issues.

Between the April, 1969 NSSM and the January, 1970 meeting of the Under Secretaries Committee, the State Department intensified its efforts to reach a compromise acceptable to both sides. To accommodate the interests of both Defense and Interior, the State Department proposed the adoption of an intermediate zone in the disputed area between the 200-meter isobath and the outer edge of the continental margin. In this zone, the coastal nation would enjoy control over the exploration and exploitation of seabed resources. While responsible for enforcing standards to protect against pollution and navigation hazards, the coastal nation would not have the right to exclude other nations from conducting scientific research or military activities on the continental margin beyond the 200-meter isobath. The State Department compromise further

[24] The date of the Seabed NSSM given by John P. Leacocos is April 11, 1969. See his "Kissinger's Apparat," *Foreign Policy*, vol. 5 (Winter, 1971–72), p. 25.

stipulated that a small royalty—2 percent of the value of resources exploited in the zone—would be paid to an international community fund.

The Department of State's compromise proposal was given a mixed reception. While the Interior Department did not object to it strenuously, Defense Department representatives rejected it flatly. Defense argued that an intermediate zone would be temporary at best and that giving the coastal state exclusive jurisdiction over resource exploitation on its continental margin would jeopardize the freedom of other nations to use that area for other purposes. Explicit guarantees of access for military or scientific purposes, Defense argued, would simply not be acceptable to coastal nations. Only by combining a narrow continental shelf with a generous international regime would there be any chance of halting the proliferation of unilateral national claims.

The NSC System and White House Intervention

With this final failure to reach agreement, the Under Secretaries Committee meeting was scheduled for January 29, 1970, and the major contenders began to recruit allies within other parts of the bureaucracy. Interior consolidated the backing of the Commerce Department and won the added support of the Bureau of the Budget and John Ehrlichman, the president's domestic affairs advisor. The Defense Department found backing within the Justice Department and the National Security Council (while continuing to lobby in the State Department for a revision of its proposal). And, in back of its intermediate zone proposal, the State Department lined up the Transportation Department and the National Science Foundation.

Given the power of the major antagonists—the petroleum industry and the military—allies seemed scarcely necessary to ensure that the Under Secretaries Committee would not render a judgment adverse to either party. In any case, under the NSC options system the committee did not have the power to impose a decision. Chaired by then-Under Secretary of State Elliot Richardson, the committee's mandate was limited to submitting a report to Presidential Assistant Henry Kissinger, for review and consideration by the president.[25] The result of the meeting, therefore, was a foregone conclusion. While the pros and cons of the Departments of State, Interior, and Defense positions were discussed heatedly, they were not resolved. The only decision taken was to send the policy dispute further up the NSC ladder with Under Secretary Richardson's recommendation accompanied by position papers from the dissenting agencies.[26]

In the month and a half following the Under Secretaries Committee meeting, the Defense Department and its supporters mounted a particularly vigorous campaign against the State Department position. In response to these objections and in his capacity as chairman of the Under Secretaries

[25] For a description of the role and stature of the Under Secretaries Committee in the National Security Council Committee hierarchy, see Hedrick Smith, "Foreign Policy: Kissinger at Hub," *New York Times,* January 19, 1971, p. 1; James Reston, "The Kissinger Role," *New York Times,* March 3, 1971, p. 39.

[26] The Under Secretaries Committee meeting, the positions of the protagonists and outcome are described in Edward Wenk, Jr., *The Politics of the Ocean* (Seattle: University of Washington Press, 1972), pp. 274 ff.

Committee, Elliot Richardson proposed a fourth policy position on the continental shelf boundary and the seabed regime. The new policy was an obvious compromise between the State Department position on an intermediate zone and the Defense Department position in favor of a narrow continental shelf. In his proposal Richardson suggested that the concept of the intermediate zone be retained but that the zone be expressly incorporated into the international regime. The proposal went on to stipulate that, within the intermediate zone, the coastal state would have the exclusive right to grant concessions and to collect royalties as a "trustee" of the international community. Substantial royalties from exploitation in the zone would be allocated to international economic development. Richardson's proposal differed from the original State Department position on the outer limit of the national continental shelf boundary and the size of royalties to be allocated to the international community. It promptly superceded the Department of State's earlier proposal and became the official departmental position.

The reactions of both the Defense and Interior Departments to the revised State Department position were revealing. The Defense Department continued to prefer its own concept of preferential bidding rights for coastal nations, but it deemed the new proposal acceptable as a "fall-back" position since it explicitly stipulated that national sovereignty would end at the 200-meter isobath and since it stressed the international character of the trusteeship zone. Interior Department officials were far less sanguine about Richardson's proposal. Interior's main objection was to the provisions that would give the international community discretionary authority in the intermediate zone and would only accord the coastal state the role of "trustee." Such authority would mean that the international community, of which developing nations constitute a majority, would have the power to decide upon and to impose production controls, to fix high royalty payments, to impose other onerous restrictions upon the coastal state, or to exclude the coastal state altogether from its trusteeship zone. Finally, the Interior Department expressed concern that the Richardson proposal, unlike the earlier State Department position, called for a large amount in royalties to be paid to an international fund. The Interior Department urged, therefore, a return to the abandoned State Department policy on the shelf boundary and a seabed regime.

With the formulation of the Richardson proposal and the retention of the original State Department proposal at the insistence of Interior, there were four policy options to be considered by the White House.[27] Although these were sent to the president in March, no decision on the options was forthcoming until the end of May. The paramount cause of delay was the fact that the continental shelf/seabed regime issue had to compete with more urgent matters for the time and attention of busy presidential advisors. The U.S. invasion of Cam-

[27] On the agency positions that were considered by the president, see: Jerry Landauer, "Nixon is Urged to Yield Some Ocean Floor Oil to Help the World's Poor," *Wall Street Journal,* March 27, 1970, p. 1; U.S., Congress, Senate, Committee on Interior and Insular Affairs, *Outer Continental Shelf, Hearings,* Part II, 1970, pp. 361 ff.; Samuel C. Orr, "Domestic Pressures Quicken US Policymaking on Seabed Jurisdiction," *CPR National Journal,* March 28, 1970, pp. 676 ff.

bodia was such a case. A fundamental and recurring source of delay, however, was the difficulty for White House officials of mastering the complex technical and legal issues of the seabed question. Kissinger was particularly reluctant to involve himself in a subject with which he had had little experience. Hence the problem was shoved aside.

This state of affairs might have persisted indefinitely had not other White House principals intervened in the agency dispute. Because the continental shelf/seabed regime problem spans domestic as well as foreign policy considerations, Interior Department officials directly solicited the support of John Ehrlichman, the president's advisor for domestic affairs. Unlike Kissinger, Ehrlichman was quite prepared to take a position on this question after an initial briefing by Interior Department officials. Ehrlichman was concerned that an executive branch policy in support of a narrow continental shelf would expose the president to the politically damaging charge of "giving away" the nation's mineral estate. Therefore, Ehrlichman opted for either the Interior Department or the original State Department position. Officials of the National Security Council received Ehrlichman's intervention in a matter of foreign policy with less than complete enthusiasm. They were concerned that American strategic interests would be gravely endangered by the broad continental shelf policies of the Interior and original State Department positions. Thus the lines were firmly drawn between the president's foreign and domestic affairs advisors and the issue was once again stalled.[28]

[28] U.S., Congress, Senate, Committee on Interior and Insular Affairs, *Outer Continental Shelf, Hearings,* Part II, 1970, p. 399. On the operation of these two power centers in the White

At this point external events combined to force strenuous efforts within the White House to negotiate a mutually acceptable options paper for the president. While the UN Seabed Committee was pressing ahead with its deliberations, a growing number of countries were laying claim to extensive offshore jurisdictions—Brazil to a 200-mile territorial sea and Canada to a 100-mile pollution safety zone.[29] At the same time, news of the interagency dispute was leaking to Congress and the press.[30] The Senate Interior and Insular Affairs Committee was threatening to hold hearings which would have exposed the interagency dispute and to issue a report on its own in the absence of a prompt presidential decision.[31]

House, see Robert B. Semple, Jr., "Nixon's Style as Boss Combines Desire for Order and Solitude," *New York Times,* January 12, 1970, p. 1.

[29] "Secret Crisis," *Wall Street Journal,* March 20, 1970, p. 1.

[30] Examples include: Landauer, "Nixon Urged to Yield Ocean Floor Oil," *Wall Street Journal,* March 27, 1970, p. 1; Orr, "Domestic Pressures Quicken US Policymaking," *CPR National Journal,* March 28, 1970, pp. 676 ff.; "Oceans of Oil," *National Observer,* April 6, 1970, p. 12.

[31] Unwilling to have the agency dispute aired publicly, the White House sent John Whittaker, a member of the president's staff, to ask Senator Metcalf for more time to reach a unified government position. Senator Metcalf agreed to postpone the hearings from April 8 to April 22. The intra-White House disagreement, however, was not easily resolved and on April 17, Senator Metcalf was once again asked to delay the hearings. The senator agreed but made it clear that in the absence of a Presidential decision, his Subcommittee would issue a report on its own. In a letter dated April 28, Kenneth BeLieu, Deputy Assistant to the President, pledged that the Administration would present a unified position to the Subcommittee on May 27. U.S., Congress, Senate, Senator Metcalf Speaking on the Seaward Limit of our Legal Continental Shelf, 91st cong., 2nd sess., April 13, 1970, *Congressional Record,* daily ed., p. S5590; Senate, Committee on Interior and Insular Affairs, *Outer Continental Shelf, Hearings,* Part II, pp. 423–27.

The challenge, therefore, was to prepare an options memorandum for the president that was acceptable to both Ehrlichman and Kissinger. The NSC staff drafted a series of memoranda for review and comment by the domestic affairs staff. Of paramount concern to Ehrlichman in the first NSC drafts was the omission of the original State Department position as one of the options to go to the president. It was that position, in Ehrlichman's view, that offered the best compromise between domestic and foreign policy considerations. The Defense Department position did not ensure national control over the valuable petroleum resources of the U.S. continental margin. The Interior Department position, on the other hand, ignored the problem of creeping jurisdiction. And, in a contest between the Richardson and the first State Department positions, Ehrlichman preferred the latter since it recognized the inherent legal rights of states to the resources of their continental margins.

The Ehrlichman views were taken into account in the final version of the option paper that was sent to the president over Kissinger's signature at the end of April. The NSC staff, however, was responsible for the structuring of the memorandum, giving it an obvious advantage in determining the president's decision. After setting out the four agency positions and their rationales and after explaining Ehrlichman's support for the original State Department position, the Kissinger memorandum concluded with the recommendation that the president choose the Defense or the Richardson option. The Richardson position thereby became the obvious middle position; the one which the president ultimately adopted.

After months of delay while the issue had made its way to the White House, the president's decision was made after only brief consideration and on the basis of a carefully constructed set of options. Once President Nixon selected the Richardson option, the NSC system again took over. In cooperation with the State Department, the victorious agency, the NSC staff drafted a National Security Decision Memorandum conveying the president's decision to the heads of all interested federal agencies. The NSDM not only outlined the principles that were to govern a prospective treaty to be submitted to the United Nations Seabed Committee but it also specified that the State Department would be responsible for preparing the treaty, the U.S. negotiating position, and the necessary legislative measures, in coordination with the Departments of Defense and Interior.

The stipulation that the State Department coordinate its efforts to negotiate a Seabed Treaty with both Interior and Defense confirmed the fact that the NSC system reserved all critical or disputed foreign policy issues for White House decision. From the time of the June, 1969 National Security Study Memorandum, the State Department had been effectively precluded from making an independent decision on the seabed regime over the opposition of the affected agencies. The January, 1970 meeting of the Under Secretaries Committee was one further step in the progress of the decision to the White House. Elliot Richardson, chairman of the committee, did not have the authority under the NSC system to impose a decision. His recommendation went to the president as one of several options advanced by the dissenting agencies. As they reached the president, the options were carefully structured and articulated by Kissinger's staff, with the intervention in this instance of Ehrlichman. At the top of the pyramid was the president, advised by Kissinger to adopt the Richardson or the Defense option. The success of the Richardson position lay as much in its presentation as in its intrinsic merit or persuasiveness. No doubt Kissinger's and Nixon's personal rapport with Richardson also played an important role in their choice.

While the NSC options system reserved the key or disputed ocean policy decisions for the White House, the implementation of those decisions was left to lower level bureaucrats. Important power, thereby, remained in the hands of the technicians who had mastered the legal, geological, strategic and economic complexities of ocean issues.

With the issuance of the May 22 NSDM, the task of announcing and then implementing the president's decision returned to the bureaucracy. The "president's seabed policy" was announced by legal advisor John Stevenson and Ronald Zeigler at a White House press conference on May 23.[32] The public was told that the president was calling for the renunciation of national claims to seabed resources beyond the depth of 200 meters and for the establishment, beyond this point, of an international regime to govern the exploitation of seabed resources. Two types of machinery would be created to authorize resource exploitation in this international seabed area. To the edge of the continental margin, an area called the "trusteeship zone," the coastal state would administer exploitation as a trustee for the

[32] White House Press Release, News Conference no. 607, "United States Policy for the Seabed," *Weekly Compilation of Presidential Documents,* vol. 6 (1970), p. 677; also in U.S., *Department of State Bulletin,* LXII, June 15, 1970, pp. 737–38.

international community. In return the "coastal state would receive a share of the international revenues from the zone in which it acts as trustee." Beyond the continental margin, international machinery would authorize and regulate exploitation and would collect "substantial mineral royalties" to be used for economic assistance to developing countries. In addition the international regime would formulate "rules to prevent unreasonable interference with other uses of the ocean, to protect the ocean from pollution, to assure the integrity of the investment necessary for such exploitation, and to provide for peaceful and compulsory settlement of disputes."

The May 23 statement, Elliot Richardson informed the Congress, represented only an initial "approach to dealing with the exploitation of the continental margin." The president promised that the executive would introduce more specific proposals at the UN Seabed Committee meeting scheduled in August, 1970.[33] During that summer a five-man drafting committee prepared a convention of 78 articles and five appendices. The ad hoc group included Bernard Oxman of the Legal Advisor's Office, Louis Sohn and Stuart McIntyre, also from the State Department, Leigh Ratiner with the Defense Department, and Vincent McKelvey of the Interior Department. Although drafted in some secrecy, early versions of the treaty were shown to private industry[34] and the Congress. Due to the

[33] U.S., Congress, Senate, Committee on Interior and Insular Affairs, *Outer Continental Shelf, Hearings,* Part II, 1970, pp. 430–35.

[34] During the week of July 9–14, 1970, representatives of the National Petroleum Council, American Petroleum Institute, Standard of New Jersey, Kennecott Copper, Union Carbide, and Deep Sea Ventures met with the drafting committee to

strenuous opposition of these groups and the Interior Department to many of the treaty provisions, some modifications were made.[35] On August 3, the first day of the meeting, the United States presented a "United Nations Draft Convention on the International Seabed Area." This lengthy and complex draft quickly became the cornerstone of U.S. seabed policy. The most significant modification of this policy has been in the U.S. position on the trusteeship zone—the acceptance of exclusive coastal state jurisdiction over the resources of the continental margin. Before turning to consider the reception of the U.S. treaty in the United States and at the United Nations, as well as the forces that led to this modification, it is useful to consider separate but related early developments in law of the sea policy—in

---

review early versions of the draft treaty. Most vocal in its opposition to its provisions was the petroleum industry. *Ocean Science News,* vol. 12, no. 30, July 24, 1970, p. 1.

[35] On June 29 Senator Metcalf requested that a copy of the draft treaty be sent to his Subcommittee and subsequently expressed grave doubts to Secretary of State Rogers about many of its provisions. The Subcommittee urged that it be revised and not be presented at Geneva. In an effort to accommodate these objections, officials from the Departments of State, Defense and Interior met in executive session on July 27 with members of the Subcommittee. Changes made in the text of the draft included a downward revision of the percentage of fees to be paid from the international trusteeship area, the reduction of the status of the draft treaty to a working paper, and the addition of a stipulation that the appendices were included solely by way of example. U.S., Congress, Senate, Committee on Interior and Insular Affairs, *Outer Continental Shelf, Hearings,* Part II, p. 463 and *Outer Continental Shelf, Report,* p. 25; Samuel C. Orr, "Soviet, Latin Opposition Blocks Agreement on Seabeds Treaty," *CPR National Journal,* September 12, 1970, pp. 197 ff.; "The U.S. Should Not Present a Seabed Treaty at Geneva," *Ocean Science News,* vol. 12, no. 30, July 24, 1970, p. 1.

the area of the territorial sea, international straits and marine fisheries.

Territorial Sea, Straits and Fisheries: 1970–1973

A principal strategy behind the 1970 U.S. seabed proposal was to encourage other nations to adopt a narrow continental shelf policy. It was also hoped, at least by Defense Department officials, that the seabed proposal would have a positive effect on separate negotiations then underway regarding the breadth of the territorial sea,[36] transit through international straits, and fisheries. Discussions with the Soviets on territorial seas and straits first began in 1967. In subsequent negotiations with U.S. allies and, through 1971, at the United Nations, questions of territorial sea, straits, and fisheries were grouped as a "manageable" negotiating package. The official U.S. policy of keeping this tripartite "package" separate from continental shelf and seabed issues reflected bureaucratic factors as well as tactical considerations. Within each government agency active in ocean policy, separate offices had traditionally handled these two sets of issues. Important in reinforcing this division was the preference of government officials for neat packages of tradeoffs—a narrow continental shelf for a generous seabed regime and freedom of transit through and over international straits in exchange for a 12-mile territorial sea with preferential coastal state fishing rights in the area beyond. In both packages, strategic

[36] Within the area of the territorial sea, the littoral state exercises full sovereign jurisdiction, except for the right of innocent passage.

considerations were accorded priority over resource interests. And in practice the division of issues was never absolute.

In the course of 1971 and 1972, this division of issues, and the tradeoffs thereby implied, gradually disappeared. Domestic and international pressures were working against the official U.S.-supported grouping of tradeoffs. First, domestic interests were becoming more active in the formulation of ocean policy. As this involvement increased, the priority formerly accorded U.S. strategic considerations over resource interests decreased. Secondly, and at cross purposes with domestic pressures, foreign nations were pressing for a single international conference to consider all ocean issues.[37] Developing countries were hopeful that by combining and then trading on the whole range of law of the sea questions, they would gain greater concessions from the maritime nations.

Before these pressures prevailed, however, the U.S. handled the straits, territorial sea, and fisheries issues as a single entity. The first public announcement of the policy on territorial sea, straits, and fisheries was made in February, 1970. The United States position as elaborated by John Stevenson was that it was prepared to recognize a 12-mile territorial sea only if freedom of transit through and

[37] General Assembly Resolution 2574A (December 15, 1969) called on the Secretary General to poll the membership on the desirability of calling a conference to discuss all law of the sea regimes. Opposed by the U.S. and the Soviet Union, it passed by a vote of 65 in favor, 12 opposed, and 30 abstaining. General Assembly Resolution 2750C (December 17, 1970) called for a third UN Conference on the Law of the Sea and identified seabed, straits, territorial seas, and fisheries as potential agenda items.

over international straits were to be guaranteed by international agreement.[38] If the breadth of the territorial sea were universally extended to 12 miles, 116 international straits would be covered by territorial waters.[39] In these straits high seas corridors would cease to exist and transit would be subject to the regime of innocent passage.[40] To avoid the application of coastal state discretion to these vessels, it was necessary to guarantee the right of freedom of transit.

Although the Soviets adopted a 12-mile territorial sea in 1927, they have since become a maritime power with global interests. They have therefore fully supported the U.S. position on freedom

[38] John R. Stevenson, Speech to Philadelphia Bar Association and Philadelphia World Affairs Council, February 18, 1970, Press Release 49, U.S., Department of State *Bulletin,* March 16, 1970, p. 314; Press Release 64, U.S., Department of State *Bulletin,* March 16, 1970, p. 343; U.S., Department of Defense, "United States Policy with Respect to Territorial Sea," U.S., Department of Defense Press Release, February 25, 1970.

[39] There is disagreement on this number. The more-or-less official U.S. government figure is 116. A chart prepared by the geographer of the State Department for the 1958 UN Conference (entitled "World Straits Affected by a Twelve Mile Territorial Sea") lists 121. The State Department Pamphlet *Sovereignty of the Sea* (Geographic Bulletin No. 3, Revised October, 1969) includes 94 candidates between seven and 24 miles.

[40] The right of innocent passage through territorial waters is exercised subject to compliance with the regulations of the coastal state. In practice it may be considerably restricted. Submarines are required to navigate on the surface of territorial waters; the right of warships to passage without express consent is widely disputed; and no provision is made for innocent passage of aircraft, thereby precluding all rights to fly over territorial seas. See United Nations, Conference on the Law of the Sea, Convention on the Territorial Sea and the Contiguous Zone, Articles 14 to 23, UN Doc. A/CONF.13/L52 (April 29, 1958).

of transit through and over international straits. The interests of the Japanese and Soviets, however, diverge from those of the United States over fisheries. The second and third largest fishing nations of the world respectively, the Japanese and Soviets were not in accord with the preferential fishing rights the United States was prepared to grant to coastal nations dependent on their offshore fisheries. U.S. proposals on fishing, however, were designed to appease coastal rather than distant water fishing interests. By the late 1960s, nine Latin American nations had claimed zones of 200 miles to protect fishery resources off their shores. To halt the trend toward such claims and to induce these nations to roll back established claims, the United States proposed that special or preferential rights over offshore living resources be granted to coastal nations. According to the concept of preferential rights, a coastal fishing nation would be able to reserve a portion of the catch off its shores for its own fishermen.[41] The amount would be determined by the coastal state's economic dependence on or extent of investment in offshore fisheries. At the insistence of the Department of Defense, this proposal deliberately avoided the concept of a fishing zone that might subsequently evolve into a fixed area of expanded coastal state jurisdiction.[42]

Among fishing nations the United States ranks sixth and, although its fleets fish off the shores of

[41] Leigh S. Ratiner, "United States Oceans Policy: An Analysis," *Journal of Maritime Law and Commerce,* January, 1971, pp. 248–49.

[42] U.S., Congress, House, Committee on Armed Services, *Territorial Sea Boundaries, Hearings* before the Subcommittee on Seapower (H.A.S.C. No. 91–61), June 25, 1970, p. 9291.

other nations, the bulk of its catch comes from North American coastal areas. U.S. proposals with regard to preferential rights, therefore, were detrimental to only some domestic fishing interests. U.S. fisheries policy, however, had been determined by external rather than domestic considerations—by the need to balance Soviet and Japanese distant water fishing interests with the coastal interests of developing countries and by the need to persuade the latter to accept a 12-mile territorial sea and freedom of transit through straits.

Reasons for the lack of policy input by the U.S. fishing industry in 1970 were twofold. First, the fishing industry, unlike the petroleum industry, simply did not know that discussions affecting its interests were underway within and between governments and that the Department of Defense was intent on determining the U.S. fisheries position in exchange for concessions on straits and the territorial sea.[43] The second problem hampering industry policy input was that of internal differences in the industry—between coastal and distant water fishing interests. Although John Stevenson's reference to preferential fishing rights in his February 1970 speech was quite sketchy, it was sufficient to alarm the distant water fishing segments of the U.S. fishing industry. The reaction of their representatives to a preferential rights approach was similar to that of the Soviet Union and Japan. The U.S. coastal fishermen, on the other hand, shared the interests of developing coastal countries in obtaining preferential rights to offshore resources.

[43] David C. Loring, "The United States-Peruvian 'Fisheries' Dispute," *Stanford Law Review*, vol. 23 (February, 1971), p. 429.

Neither segment of the industry, however, appreciated being excluded from the policy deliberations. Despite intra-industry differences both segments recognized that if they were to have any influence on U.S. fisheries policy, they would have to act in concert.[44]

In order to gain a voice in policy formulation the fishing industry began to exert pressure on a number of fronts in 1971. With congressional support, two executive branch voices for the industry gradually strengthened their positions vis à vis other actors in the law of the sea policy process. In the State Department, Ambassador Donald McKernan, Special Assistant to the Secretary for Fisheries and Wildlife, was appointed the Coordinator for Marine Affairs in January, 1971. The creation of the National Oceanic and Atmospheric Administration in the Commerce Department in 1970 had seen the transfer of Interior's Bureau of Commercial Fisheries to NOAA's National Marine Fisheries Service. No longer having to compete with petroleum interests for the attention of top officials in Interior, fisheries interests, through NOAA officials, were able to play a larger role in LOS fisheries policy. The industry has exerted leverage on the Congress not only at the state level but also through its various Washington offices and through the Washington National Fisheries Institute. When a private Advisory Group on Law of the Sea was formed in

[44] U.S., Congress, Senate, Senator Hatfield on Fish Industry Representation at United Nations Conference, December 13, 1971, *Congressional Record,* daily ed., S21555; Senator Hatfield on the U.S. Fishing Industry, November 20, 1971, *Congressional Record* S19908; U.S., Congress, House, Congressman Pelly on a Program to Conserve World Fishery Resources, December 7, 1971, *Congressional Record,* daily ed., E. 13076.

1972, the industry mobilized its Congressional support to wangle two seats on the U.S. delegation for its fisheries subcommittee. While the extra seat reflects continuing differences between coastal, anadramous and distant water interests, the desire for a voice in the policy process has promoted a degree of cooperation.

The adoption of the "species approach" as official U.S. policy was the most notable product of industry cooperation. It was first elaborated, together with the U.S. position on straits and territorial seas, on July 30, 1971, before the UN Seabed Committee.[45] The species approach applied the concept of preferential rights for the coastal state beyond an exclusive fishing zone of up to 12 miles to coastal and anadromous stocks of fish. Coastal states would not have preferential rights to highly migratory oceanic species such as tuna, thereby protecting the U.S. fleets fishing off the west coast of Latin America. To provide for U.S., Soviet, and Japanese fishing off the shores of other nations—at least temporarily—the U.S. proposed that the fishing capacity of a coastal state be used to determine the extent of its preferential rights in its offshore fishery. As that capacity expanded, so would the coastal nation's preferential rights, leaving, of course, the problem of how to phase out fishing efforts of other nations in the area. To deal with this and other problems the U.S. proposal included provisions for international cooperation in inspection and dispute settlement as well as joint conservation measures to prevent overfishing. Only if all other

[45] United Nations, General Assembly, UN Doc. A/AC.138/ SC.II/L.4 (1971); also available in *International Legal Materials,* vol. 10, 1971, p. 1018.

measures failed was unilateral state action deemed acceptable. Like the 1970 U.S. seabed proposal, the U.S. species approach of 1971 envisioned a strong role for international and regional organizations in the regulation of high seas resources and sought thereby to reduce pressure for unilateral extension of coastal state control over offshore resources.

As elaborated in 1971 and as revised in 1972, the species approach represented an effort to accommodate U.S. fisheries policy to the prevailing trend toward resource zones of up to 200 miles. Canada's expanded fishery closing lines had gone into effect in February, 1971. Brazil had applied restrictive fishing measures to a distance of 200 miles.[46] Most significantly, even Malta's Ambassador Pardo had spoken out in favor of a 200-mile resource zone.[47] Within the government the issue of fisheries received a great deal of attention throughout 1971. The viability of applying the trusteeship concept to fishery resources or alternatively of accepting functional or resource zones was the subject of a National Security Study Memorandum soliciting agency responses. The objective of this review was to straighten out U.S. policy priorities among the diverse issues under consideration by the United Nations Seabed Committee. The apparent result of the review was to disentangle fisheries from other considerations.

[46] In spring, 1972 the U.S. and Brazil reached agreement on a treaty that temporarily settled the conflict over U.S. shrimp fishing while allowing both parties to avoid recognition of the other's claims.

[47] United Nations, General Assembly, UN Doc. A/AC.138/53 (March 23, 1971).

In August, 1972, when the U.S. next introduced draft articles on fisheries to the UN Seabed Committee,[48] they were no longer linked to territorial sea and straits policy. In the fisheries articles as well as in seabed policy statements, there were further concessions granting the coastal state jurisdiction over offshore resources. U.S. distant water fishing interests played a role in drafting the article, as evidenced by retention of the species approach,[49] but majority international sentiment for wide fishing zones was also a major factor behind the 1972 revisions in U.S. fisheries policy. The new articles provided that the coastal state would regulate harvesting of coastal and anadromous species and that international fisheries organizations would regulate highly migratory stocks. The coastal state had the right to reserve to its flag vessels all the stocks it could harvest. Above that level and to the point of scientifically determined maximum sustainable yield, the coastal state would grant access to other fishing states with priority to those historically fishing the area and then to other states in the region. As its own fishing capacity increased, the coastal state would reduce the amount of catch allocated to the other states.

The U.S. position on fisheries was reiterated in 1973 with no significant changes in substance. Then at the Caracas meeting of the Law of the Sea Conference, the United States accepted a 200-mile resource zone. The U.S. tabled draft articles on the

[48] United Nations, General Assembly, UN Doc. A/AC.138/SC.II/L.9 (1972).

[49] John Neary, "Chaos at Sea III," *Saturday Review/World,* December 4, 1973, p. 20.

economic zone and the continental shelf providing for exclusive coastal state rights to exploitation and regulation of fishing within the zone.[50] These articles maintained the U.S. position on the need for full utilization of coastal stocks, access for traditional fishing states to stocks the coastal state is unable to harvest, and special provision for anadromous and highly migratory species.

Unlike the U.S. position on fisheries, that on straits and territorial seas has remained essentially unchanged since its initial statement in the 1970 Stevenson speech and its presentation to the Seabed Committee as draft articles in July, 1971. The articles provided for a territorial sea breadth of up to a maximum of 12 miles with baselines to be determined in accordance with criteria set out in the 1958 Geneva Convention on the Territorial Sea and Contiguous Zone. In straits used for international navigation, all ships and aircraft would enjoy a high seas freedom of navigation. While coastal states would have the right to designate corridors suitable for transit, those corridors customarily employed would have to be included and international traffic safety regulations would be agreed. In the statement accompanying these articles, Stevenson indicated that the United States was prepared to accept a 12-mile limit *if* the right of free transit were provided for all vessels and aircraft through and over international straits. Stevenson stressed that free transit was "a limited but vital right" and added that the

[50] United Nations, Third Conference on the Law of the Sea, *United States of America: Draft Articles for a Chapter on the Economic Zone and the Continental Shelf,* UN Doc. A/CONF. 62/C.2/L.47 (1974).

right was merely one of "transiting the straits, not of conducting any other activities."

During 1971 a number of personnel changes occurred in the Defense Department. With David Packard's departure from government, law of the sea responsibilities were transferred from the Legal Counsel's Office to the Offices of the Joint Chiefs of Staff and International Security Affairs (ISA). At the same time, the issue rose to such prominence within DOD that Secretary of Defense Melvin Laird and Secretary of the Navy John Warner began to take a direct interest in law of the sea negotiations. As the U.S. position on the continental shelf and fisheries gradually evolved toward coastal state rights and jurisdiction in a 200-mile zone, these officials attached even greater importance to unimpeded straits transit. Defense officials were convinced of the importance to national security of global mobility and viewed as unacceptable any law of the sea treaty which did not guarantee freedom of transit over international straits.

If 1971 was the year of fish in U.S. government deliberations, 1972 was the year of straits. As noted above, the U.S. proposal on straits was linked in 1971 to U.S. fisheries policy, but not by 1972. While there was wide support in the UN in 1971 for a 12-mile territorial sea, there was little support for the straits proposal. Opposition to freedom of transit centered initially in the Spanish delegation and evolved by 1972 to become the focal point of domestic and international contention.

As accusations of intransigence were being hurled at the U.S. delegation at the spring, 1972 session of the Seabed Committee, other U.S. interests became alarmed at the prospects for a successful law of the sea conference. Officials from the Departments of State and Interior pressed for National Security Studies of alternative straits policies hoping to modify, if not overrule, the Defense position on straits. With the personal involvement of Secretary Laird, however, the Defense view prevailed in the White House evaluation of alternative policies presented to it. The NSDM issued to the U.S. delegation in the summer of 1972 contained no modification of the U.S. freedom of transit policy.

The firm U.S. stand on straits led to an impasse at the August, 1972 meeting of the Seabed Committee. Developing nations, organized as the "Group of 77," had submitted an agenda for the LOS Conference containing no provision for freedom of transit through straits. Following several weeks of hard bargaining, the chairman of the Seabed Committee, Hamilton S. Amerasinghe, proposed the compromise formulation "right of transit" as the straits agenda item. While other delegations waited, the head of the U.S. delegation cabled Washington on August 11 for a change in instructions to accept the compromise. The Departments of Interior and Commerce, concerned with seeing their own interests advanced in the international negotiations, supported the State Department in requesting the change. Only Defense remained steadfastly opposed. Meeting three days later in Washington, agency officials were still unable to agree and John Irwin, chairman of the Under Secretaries Committee, was forced to take the dispute to the White House. With Kissinger en route to Saigon and the president in San Clemente, it took over seven days to press the change in delegation instructions to a resolution. The decision taken favored the compromise formula, "right of transit" overruling the Defense Department and making possible completion of the Seabed Committee's work on an agenda at the fall, 1972 session.

Despite this seeming concession in a situation of negotiating impasse, there has in fact been no shift in the government position and certainly no new treaty articles have been submitted. In contrast to 1972, 1973 was a quiet year on the straits problem as the spotlight shifted to negotiations on the seabed regime, marine pollution, and scientific research. The most significant developments for U.S. straits policy in 1973 and 1974 stem from the war in the Middle East and the "energy crisis." The paramount lesson of the Middle East conflict, in Defense Department eyes, was the inability to rely on NATO allies for refueling and overflight rights in the event of a conflict they do not support. An internationally guaranteed right of access through international straits was obviously indispensable to a limited military action. The lesson of the subsequent "energy crisis," as Defense has chosen to interpret it, is the need to protect transport of vital commodities and therefore to keep sea lanes open.

Seabed Policy: 1971–1974

With the tabling of the U.S. draft treaty at the August, 1970 Geneva meeting, domestic industry opposition to the treaty merged with and was buttressed by the reflex United Nations sentiment against policy initiatives of major powers. Quickly marshalling their forces in 1971, industry deftly directed their arguments at the lengthy and complex draft treaty rather than at the president's May 23 statement. Objections to the treaty were of two types: (1) petroleum industry opposition to relinquishing coastal state jurisdiction beyond the 200-meter isobath [51] and (2) hard minerals industry opposition to the mining provisions elaborated in the treaty and its annexes.[52]

In the absence of significant international support for the draft treaty,[53] the official U.S. position gradually evolved toward accepting some form of coastal state economic resource zone. By August of 1972, U.S. representatives were emphasizing for the first time a strong U.S. interest in offshore resources.[54] Noting widespread support for an economic zone of 200 miles, Stevenson indicated that the U.S. would accept coastal state regulation of the exploitation of mineral resources subject to international standards and compulsory settlement of disputes. Other uses of the area were not to be restricted and pollution controls were to be internationally determined. Revenues from seabed resources would be shared with the international community and foreign investment in the area would be

[51] National Petroleum Council, *Petroleum Resources Under the Ocean Floor,* Supplemental Report, Washington, D.C., March 4, 1971.

[52] T. S. Ary, *Statement of American Mining Congress to the Department of the Interior with Respect to Working Paper of the Draft United Nations Convention on the International Seabed Area,* Washington, D.C., January 27, 1971.

[53] The developing landlocked and shelf-locked nations that would be the obvious beneficiaries of a narrow national continental shelf and a generous international regime beyond, encountered great ideological barriers to lending their support to a U.S. proposal.

[54] United Nations, General Assembly, Statement of John R. Stevenson, UN Doc. A/AC.138/SR.77–89 at p. 63 (August 10, 1972). See also, *United States Foreign Policy for the 1970's,* a Report by President Richard Nixon to the Congress, May 3, 1973, p. 217.

protected from expropriation. In 1973 the U.S. introduced draft treaty articles incorporating these provisos and granting the coastal state exclusive rights to seabed resources in an area yet to be determined.[55] In the articles presented at Caracas, the U.S. proposed that the area be defined as extending to the limit of the economic zone or beyond that to the outer limit of the continental margin.

While Government policy has evolved since 1970 toward the position of the petroleum industry, the industry's position has changed from outspoken unilateralism to support for international standards and regulations. Though not embracing an international authority to license the petroleum resources of the margin, the industry does support the creation of an international tribunal possibly affiliated with an international deep seabed authority. After a strong attack on the U.S. draft treaty in March, 1971,[56] the petroleum industry refrained from further official comments on the subject of offshore jurisdiction until December, 1972. During this period, industry representatives lobbied in favor of a broad national continental shelf, and received a warm response from those coastal nations inclined to broad offshore jurisdiction.

As ocean interests of the petroleum industry became more diverse, a single petroleum policy became increasingly difficult to determine. Whereas domestic sectors of the major petroleum companies had formerly determined ocean policy in cooperation with the Interior Department and its National Petroleum

[55] United Nations, General Assembly, UN Doc. A/AC.138/SC.II/L.35 (1973), and statement of John R. Stevenson, UN Doc. A/AC.138/SC.II/SR.65 at 11 (1973).

[56] National Petroleum Council, *Petroleum Resources, Supplemental Report.*

Council, the multinational corporations, with close relations to the Department of State and elsewhere, began to play an expanding role. The involvement of new segments of the industry was reflected in changes in personnel—the disappearance of the colorful, outspoken oil man lobbying conspicuously through the Interior Department and the appearance of the oil diplomat working skillfully and quietly with the Department of State. It was also apparent in the willingness of the industry to accommodate its shipping interests to reasonable coastal state pollution controls.

These shifts were occasioned by major changes in the world environment of oil. The multinationals had begun to have their first serious difficulties with the producing nations operating as a bloc in the Organization of Petroleum Exporting Countries (OPEC). While this did not propel industry spokesmen to support an international organization controlling resources beyond 200 meters depth, it did undermine industry confidence in the view that it was safer and more profitable to deal bilaterally with foreign governments. OPEC successes in increasing revenues to producing countries, buttressed by ultimate resort to expropriation, account for the evolution of the NPC position between March, 1971 and December, 1972's summary report on the "U.S. Energy Outlook." In that report the NPC suggests that "any proposed international treaty dealing with seabed mineral resources should confirm the jurisdiction of coastal nations over . . . the mineral resources of the entire submerged continental mass off their coasts." [57] Gone is the former exhortation to

[57] National Petroleum Council, *U.S. Energy Outlook,* Summary Report, December, 1972, p. 79.

the government to *unilaterally* declare "exclusive" jurisdiction over the resources of the margin. Instead the NPC recommends that an international treaty "should provide for security of investment made in resource development in areas of the continental margin pursuant to agreement with or license from the coastal state." To assure these investments, the NPC supports transferring disputes in the area "to an international tribunal for compulsory objective decision."

The muted industry tone toward coastal state control over offshore resources was made easier by the international trend toward expansive coastal state jurisdiction. By 1972, even the U.S. government was speaking sympathetically of coastal state resource zones. And in 1974, when the U.S. defined the continental shelf as extending to the outer limit of the continental margin, the NPC Interim Report on *Ocean Petroleum Resources* indicated a willingness to settle for a 200-mile limit if that would yield broad agreement on the many issues before the law of the sea conference. In the course of achieving their victory on offshore jurisdiction, the multinationals had become concerned with the prospects for transport of petroleum in a world of expanded coastal state resource jurisdiction.

In terms of its interest in transport, the petroleum industry is in the same situation as the navy. The industry was slower, however, to respond to the implications of Canada's Arctic waters pollution legislation and to take an active interest in safeguarding transit routes. Several factors may account for this. Apparently in 1970, the problem of access to offshore resources was given priority over problems of transport. When the majors did become attentive to the problems of shipping, they expected to receive different treatment at the hands of coastal nations than military users. The petroleum industry apparently regarded it as self-evident that the shipment of petroleum products at the lowest possible cost was in the interest of all nations. Thus, as long as the industry took reasonable precautions to avoid polluting the oceans, it had no reason to fear unreasonable restrictions on oil shipping.

This sanguine view of the international community interest in facilitating the economic production and distribution of petroleum was spelled out in detail in the NPC's 1973 and 1974 reports on the oceans.[58] In those reports, the industry reiterated and elaborated its support for integrity of investment (or prompt compensation in the event of expropriation) and for compulsory dispute settlement procedures. The NPC report noted the "international community interest in unimpeded navigation" for merchant ships which could be required to comply with internationally prescribed standards. Enforcement of these standards would be the prerogative of the flag state, except in the territorial sea, and coastal states would be allowed limited enforcement rights in an area beyond the territorial sea. Clearly the industry policy as outlined in these reports is quite close to the official U.S. policies on the economic zone, marine pollution and compulsory settlement of disputes.

The hard minerals industry did not have the similar experience of seeing its views converge with government policy. Despite its strenuous opposition to the 1970 U.S. Draft Treaty on the Seabed Regime,

---

[58] National Petroleum Council, *Law of the Sea: Particular Aspects Affecting the Petroleum Industry,* May, 1973, and *Ocean Petroleum Resources: An Interim Report,* July, 1974.

the thrust of the original policy has not been modified. While the petroleum industry found its opposition to the draft treaty in harmony with the majority of coastal developing states, the objections of the hard minerals industry have run counter to the majority UN sentiment. Most developing nation delegations have come to advocate a far-reaching "enterprise" system engaging in as well as regulating mining. The mining companies, on the other hand, support policies ranging from laissez-faire to an international registry of claims. The drafters of the 1970 treaty have consequently found themselves in that fortunate position of occupying the middle ground between opposing factions.

Finding little support in the Interior Department or elsewhere in the Executive branch in 1971, the industry turned to the U.S. Congress. Several mining firms were beginning to make substantial investments in developing deep sea mining technology and by the beginning of 1972, Hughes Tool Company had started construction of its mining barge.[59] At the request of Senator Lee Metcalf (D-Mont.), the American Mining Congress drafted legislation for a seabed regime that would be more congenial to mining interests than the 1970 draft treaty. Introduced originally as S.2801 on November 2, 1971 (HR 13904, March 20, 1972), the AMC bill lapsed with the 92nd Congress. Identical legislation, however, was reintroduced in the 93rd Congress (HR 9, January 3, 1973; S 1134, March 8, 1973). This industry-sponsored legislation [60] would authorize U.S. firms to mine the deep seabed under a na-

[59] *San Diego Law Review,* vol. 9, May, 1972, p. 625.
[60] The legislation was drafted and approved by all AMC member companies with one exception.

tional licensing system until the establishment of an international regime. It provides for reciprocal recognition of similar practice by other countries and for the establishment of a fund drawn from income taxes with aid directed to less developed reciprocating states. In January, 1974, this legislation was revised in the House Merchant Marine and Fisheries Committee and introduced in the Congress as HR 12233 and S 2878.[61] Although the drafters eliminated several of the more controversial provisions, a new feature of the revised bill was the addition of January, 1976 as a trigger date for the legislation—if no international regime has been negotiated by that time.

Both domestic and international opposition to these bills has been voiced. Much of the opposition in the executive branch has centered on the provisions for a U.S. government guarantee to reimburse the licensee for any loss of investment or for increased costs incurred in a 40-year period after issuance of the license resulting from requirements or limitations imposed by a subsequently agreed international regime. Foreign as well as domestic opponents point out, moreover, that enactment of this legislation could prejudice the character of the international regime to be established through negotiations in the Seabed Committee.[62] Instead of tying the hands of the executive branch, however, the AMC legislation was turned to advantage in the international negotiations. By mid-1972, agency

[61] U.S., *Congressional Record,* daily ed., January 23, 1974, pp. S255–66.

[62] United Nations, General Assembly, Statement of Chilean representative, UN General Assembly, *Official Records,* A/AC. 138/SC.I/SR.49 (March 1972).

representatives had discussed this and possible interim legislation with officials of the technologically advanced nations—in an effort to concert policy. The hope was not fulfilled, however, that the possible resort to such legislation would hurry recalcitrant Seabed Committee delegates to negotiate an international treaty along the lines of the U.S. draft treaty. Instead, the conference was delayed to 1974 with only procedural discussions held in December, 1973. Meanwhile internationalists chaffed and international mining companies proceeded with exploration and technology development.[63]

Complicating the intra-governmental deliberations on a seabed regime was the appearance of a new participant in the LOS process in March, 1973 —the Treasury Department. Until then undisputed responsibility for deep sea mining had rested with the Interior Department. Through 1971, Interior officials accorded more attention to petroleum problems than to hard minerals considerations. Then in early 1972, Interior Department law of the sea policy was turned over to officials newly recruited from the Defense Department law of the sea staff. As petroleum interests in law of the sea were progressively accommodated, hard minerals policy consumed a larger portion of the department's interest.

While the Interior officials obviously did not relish the advent of a new agency concerned with seabed policy, other law of the sea departments were equally alarmed. Together with the Council of

---

[63] In November, 1972, Summa Corporation launched the Hughes Glomar Explorer. By September (21) 1973, the *Wall Street Journal* reported that Summa had invested about $100 million in ocean mining with Kennecott and Deep Sea Ventures (Tenneco) about $20 million each.

Economic Advisors (CEA), the Council on International Economic Policy (CIEP), and the Office of Management and Budget (OMB), Treasury brought a new perspective to bear on the entire range of law of sea policies dear to the hearts of the several agencies.[64] With regard to seabed mining, for example, the Treasury Department perspective was that in a time of resource scarcity, an international regime with discretionary authority that might be used to discourage production—such as the Enterprise system proposed by the Latin Americans— would restrict supplies and raise mineral prices, hurting consuming nations. Similarly, the 1970 draft treaty sought political gains at the expense of needed resources and economic efficiency. To attempt to generate international revenues by creating an over weighted and discretionary bureaucratic structure would simply deter exploitation and limit seabed development, thereby reducing the revenues that might ultimately be available to developing nations. The sharing of revenues from seabed mining, however, was itself a proposal that should be thoroughly reexamined. Similarly inefficient would be the encouragement of mining through guarantees against financial loss as envisioned in the AMC legislation. To encourage mining before the cost of land-based sources made the risks involved sustainable would simply subsidize development of high cost minerals at the expense of the taxpayer. On the other hand, to hinder development of seabed resources when the risks were commercially acceptable would subsidize

[64] Deborah Shapley, "Law of the Sea: Energy, Economy Spur Secret Review of US Stance," *Science,* vol. 183, no. 4122, (January 25, 1974), pp. 290–92; *Sea Breezes,* Save Our Seas newsletter, vol. 1, no. 9 (November-December, 1973).

the development of higher cost land-based minerals at the expense of the consumer.

The economic perspective brought to bear on the issue of seabed mining, reflecting the views of Secretary of the Treasury George Shultz and his deputy, William Simon, was applied to the entire range of law of the sea questions: jurisdiction over the continental shelf, transit through international straits, international standards for marine pollution, and living resources. High level involvement in the Treasury Department was ultimately successful in generating a series of government studies and policy reviews. In the aftermath of the July, 1973 NSDM providing for agency studies of the economic implications of law of the sea, evolution of U.S. policy was temporarily halted pending the outcome of the review. Thereafter, the Treasury Department applied brakes wherever new developments threatened to take U.S. policy further down the path of strictly political or strategic goals.

To apply the brakes when international negotiations were well advanced did not sit well with those agency representatives whose views had already been accommodated in U.S. policy and who had therefore developed a vested interest in seeing those interests secured in an international law of the sea treaty. One response to this state of affairs was a major bureaucratic restructuring in the Department of State. The personal involvement of Shultz and Simon as well as White House advisors Kenneth Dam and Peter Flanigan called for a corresponding level of prominence for LOS in other agencies. The State Department created a new office, D/LOS, with direct access to Deputy Secretary Kenneth Rush, the chairman of the NSC Under

Secretaries Committee. Within the office John Norton Moore was appointed chairman of the NSC Interagency Task Force on the Law of the Sea and Ambassador John R. Stevenson was appointed Head of Delegation and Special Representative of the President for the Law of the Sea Conference.

In a series of agency clashes between the 1973 spring and summer sessions of the UN Seabed Committee, the Treasury Department disputed the economic soundness of agency proposals on international pollution regulations, on licensing provisions subjecting leases beyond 200 meters depth to an international regime proviso,[65] and on the 1970 draft seabed treaty. The conflict came to a head in July when the UN Seabed delegates assembled in Geneva. When the meeting opened on July 2, 1973, the U.S. delegation was without instructions. In previous years, this situation had been a result of difficulties in getting the summer White House to sign off on agency-sponsored draft instructions. In 1973, however, there was no agency agreement on draft instructions. To break this impasse, Deputy Secretary Rush convened an Under Secretaries Committee meeting on July 9 and State, Defense, and Interior officials returned to Washington.[66] Trying to strike a middle ground, an accommodation was reached providing that existing U.S. proposals were not to be considered definitive pending completion of a thorough economic review of all aspects of law of the sea.

Meanwhile, those who were anxious to proceed

[65] See *Federal Register,* Notices, vol. 38, no. 76, April 20, 1973, p. 9839; and vol. 38, no. 212, November 5, 1973, p. 30457.

[66] Shapley, *Science,* p. 291. Memorandum to Senator Metcalf from Administrative Assistant, July, 1973.

with international negotiations were able to do so under the auspices of a decision memorandum focusing on tactical considerations such as narrowing divergent positions, drafting treaty articles, and consolidating texts. Apart from details on marine pollution, the delegation was left free to elaborate the points stressed by Stevenson in August, 1972—as long as no commitments were made on revenue sharing. Making up for lost time, the U.S. delegation issued a series of treaty proposals in rapid succession: on the Coastal Seabed Economic Area (July 16), on Protection of the Marine Environment (July 18), on Marine Scientific Research (July 20) and on Settlement of Disputes (August 22). With the exception of the proposed "chapter" on compulsory dispute settlement, the other draft articles reflected a transposition into treaty language of previous policy pronouncements. While the U.S. had indicated a position on marine pollution and scientific research in previous sessions, they were the last policy areas to be converted into treaty provisions. If the appearance of the Treasury Department as a new and powerful law of the sea actor has not reversed the direction of U.S. policies set in motion in 1970, it has at least slowed the momentum.

Marine Pollution and Scientific Research

Despite their relatively late incarnation in U.S. treaty language, marine science and marine pollution are among the oldest issues under consideration in the current law of the sea negotiations. Both were included among the law of the sea items to be dealt with in the original General Assembly resolution calling for a Third United Nations Conference on

Law of the Sea to be held in 1973.[67] While provisions regarding marine science research date back
to the 1958 Geneva Conventions, the marine pollution issue came into its own in 1969. It was then
that the tanker *Manhattan* transited the North-
west Passage, one of the factors causing Canada
to respond with its Arctic Waters Pollution Prevention Act.[68] The implications of the Canadian
legislation (with its provisions for vessel construction, navigational aids, qualification of the master,
and so on), for military as well as commercial
transit, were so severe as to raise the issue to the
president in spring of 1970.[69]

Despite the temporary salience of marine pollution problems in 1970 and the growing public appeal
of ecology, it did not appear as part of the U.S.
law of the sea policy in the UN Seabed Committee
for two years. The U.S. government preferred to
limit the issues before the committee to "manageable
packages"—leaving marine pollution to be considered by the Stockholm Conference on the International Environment and to the International Maritime Consultative Organization (IMCO). Only due
to Canadian insistence was it included in the December, 1970 General Assembly resolution as one
of the items to be addressed in the Law of the Sea
Conference.

[67] United Nations, General Assembly Resolution 2750C
(December 17, 1970).

[68] Great Britain, Bill C–202, April 8, 1970 (first reading),
Second Session, 28th Parl., 18 and 19, Eliz. 2, 1 c.17, 1969–70.

[69] For some discussion of this interaction see Hollick, Ann L.,
"Canadian-American Relations: Law of the Sea," in Annette
Baker Fox, Alfred Hero, and Joseph S. Nye, Jr., eds., "Canada
and the United States: Transnational and Transgovernmental
Relations," special issue of *International Organization,* vol. 28,
no. 4, Autumn, 1974, pp. 755–80.

Since its inception as a law of the sea issue, protection of the marine environment has constituted a further battlefield between coastal and global maritime interests. The agency protagonists, therefore have fallen into their customary roles: Defense —opposing coastal state pollution zones and insisting on exemptions from international standards for military vessels; State—preferring international standards but in favor of some accommodation of international sentiment; Interior—anxious to facilitate oil transport while assuring coastal control of the resources of the margin; Transportation—concerned with the Coast Guard antipollution enforcement responsibilities and shipping concerns; and Treasury—asking what the economic effects of international as opposed to coastal state standards might be on the costs of transport and the prices of goods to be shipped. Like other law of the sea issue areas, there has been some transition in U.S. policy from insistence on exclusive international standards and flag state enforcement to limited coastal and port state rights.

The participation of private environmental interests and the government environmental agencies was relatively late. In response to strong industry pressure, a public Advisory Committee on Law of the Sea was created in early 1972, and included, as one of its eight subgroups, a marine environment subcommittee. That subcommittee, however, had only two members until 1973 and remains one of the smallest subcommittees. Similarly, the Environmental Protection Agency and the Council on Environmental Quality appeared at the law of the sea negotiations for the first time in the summer of 1973. They were added to the Interagency Task Force during the efforts of that summer to diffuse the primacy of

Treasury and the old law of the sea agencies and to provide support for new bureaucratic players. A meeting in June, preparatory to IMCO's October, 1973 Conference, provided the occasion for yet another agency clash—this time on pollution—and prompted the direct inclusion of environmental agencies in the LOS policy process.

As the participation of strictly environmental interests is recent, their policy impact is not yet clear. In the draft articles proposed by the U.S. in July, 1973,[70] the overriding concern was to accommodate coastal state concerns while avoiding pollution zones and other potential restrictions on maritime transit. Separate provisions were made for pollution due to either seabed resource exploitation or navigation. While international standards would be developed in both cases, only with regard to exploitation would the coastal state be accorded the right to set higher standards and to enforce them beyond the territorial sea. Vessel source pollution would be subject to flag and port state enforcement, with coastal state rights limited to cases of imminent harmful damage. This policy remained the U.S. position at the Law of the Sea Conference.

The Geneva Convention on the Continental Shelf was the first major area of international law to place specific restrictions on scientific research.[71] Since 1958, the trend toward regulating marine science research has progressed within the context

[70] United Nations, General Assembly, UN Doc. A/AC.138/ SC.III/L.40 (1973). Also introductory statement of John Norton Moore summarized in United Nations, General Assembly, UN Doc. A/AC.138/SC.III/SR.41 at 2 (1973).

[71] The 1958 convention provides that coastal state consent must be obtained for research "concerning the continental shelf and undertaken there."

of the conflict between developing coastal and developed maritime states. The developing nations have made clear their wish to regulate the conduct of research in any special-purpose zones of jurisdiction off their shores. Even where the research may not be of a military or commercial nature, it benefits a developed nation more than one which is technologically backward, thereby widening the already severe development gap. The U.S. scientists' response to this strong criticism has been to reiterate the benefits of scientific research to the international community as a whole, to note the adverse repercussions for science of any legal system restricting open research in coastal areas and to attempt to address the problem of technical assistance to ensure that the benefits of scientific research do indeed accrue to the developing states off whose shores it is conducted.

With regard to other interests within the United States, the marine scientist has experienced equally intractable conflicts. Relatively powerless in the 1970 petroleum-defense contention over the breadth of the continental shelf, the narrow shelf result was nonetheless favorable to marine science. With regard to the U.S. draft seabed treaty, however, the marine scientist failed to secure special guarantees for freedom of scientific research. Following this setback, the role of the National Science Foundation in marine science policy temporarily receded. When Ambassador Donald McKernan, the State Department's Special Assistant for Fisheries and Wildlife, was appointed Marine Affairs Coordinator in January, 1971, several assistant coordinators were designated including one for marine science. The marine scientist himself only began to take a regular and direct part in the policy process in 1972 with the creation of a Freedom of Science Task Group in the Ocean Affairs Board of the National Academy of Science. This group enlisted the support of prestigious domestic and international scientific bodies. In addition, the scientific community made its needs felt regularly through its advisory seat on the U.S. delegation to the UN Seabed Committee. Then in 1973, the marine scientist gained a full-time representative within the government with NSF's creation of a position to represent marine science on the Interagency Task Force and the U.S. delegation. The State Department's Marine Affairs Coordinator also continued to represent the scientific interest in international negotiations.

U.S. policy on freedom of marine science was first spelled out in draft treaty articles in summer, 1973.[72] This was due only in part to the absence, until relatively late, of an active and organized policy input by U.S. scientists. It was also due to the relative lack of attention given to the issue in UN Seabed Committee discussions. The U.S. draft articles on marine science research stress the benefits accruing to the international community from marine science and the responsibility of the marine scientist to ensure that those benefits are enjoyed by the coastal state. The obligations of the scientist therefore include advance notification, coastal state right of participation, sharing of data and samples, open publication of the research results, assistance to the coastal state in assuring the implication of the research results and compliance with international environmental standards. Compared to that of the Soviet

[72] United Nations, General Assembly, UN Doc. A/AC.138/SC.III/L.44 (1973), and statement of Donald L. McKernan summarized in United Nations, General Assembly, UN Doc. A/AC.138/SC.III/SR.42 at 5, 16 (1973).

Union, U.S. policy on marine science goes some way toward conciliating developing countries. From the viewpoint of the developing coastal state, however, it remains far from satisfying the requirement for coastal state consent within a 200-mile zone. The prospect for marine science, as for other global maritime or distant water interests, is coastal state regulation in extensive offshore zones of jurisdiction.

The net effect of the direct policy input of all interests affected by ocean policy has been a trend toward parity between the several U.S. interests—most notably between strategic and resource interests. While there has been no change in the 1970 position on straits and territorial sea breadth, in August, 1972 the U.S. began to place new emphasis on the national interest in ocean resources. Also at the August, 1972 session, the government first indicated that it was prepared to move toward coastal state management of coastal and anadromous species rather than stressing international regulation of all fishing. Similarly, with regard to mineral resources, the U.S. position has evolved toward a coastal state approach as a result of more direct interest group involvement. The government no longer contemplates limiting national jurisdiction to the 200-meter isobath. In response to strong domestic and international pressures, the U.S. moved in 1974 to a position favoring a 200-mile economic zone in which the coastal state exercises sovereign and exclusive rights for the purpose of exploring and exploiting the renewable and non-renewable resources of the seabed, subsoil, and superjacent waters. Beyond that limit to the outer edge of the continental margin, the coastal state exercises sovereign rights over the natural resources of the seabed. These rights are to be exercised subject to international standards and compulsory settlement of disputes. Other uses of the area are not to be restricted and pollution controls are to be internationally determinded. Revenues from non-renewable seabed resources would be shared with the international community and foreign investment in the area would be protected from expropriation.

Concomitant with the trend toward parity between resource and strategic interests has been separation of issues. With the active participation of various ocean interest groups the linking of policies, implying tradeoffs between interests, has broken down. This situation has been facilitated by limited progress in the work of the UN Seabed Committee. As the conference negotiations proceed, at Caracas and Geneva, the sacrifice of some domestic interests to secure others is inevitable. Indeed a major purpose of developing countries in combining all law of the sea issues in a single conference was to increase the pressure on the maritime nations for concessions. By the August, 1972 session of the Seabed Committee, the developing nations had succeeded in expanding the conference agenda to twenty-six subjects.[73] In the face of apparently increasing parity among U.S. interests, however, seri-

---

[73] In addition to the standard items of straits, territorial seas, fisheries, the seabed regime, marine pollution and scientific research, some of the new items included: land-locked countries, rights and interests of states with broad shelves, rights and interests of shelf-locked states and states with narrow shelves or short coastlines, regional arrangements, high seas, archipelagos, enclosed and semi-enclosed seas, artificial islands and installations, the development and transfer of technology, dispute settlement, zones of peace and security, archaeological and historical treasures on the ocean floor and peaceful uses of ocean space.

71

ous negotions will have to proceed much farther before international pressures for compromise will result in the sacrifice of some facets of the U.S. position for the retention of others.

INTERNATIONAL PERSPECTIVE

The success of developing nations in expanding the number of agenda items to be considered by the conference has proven the greatest obstacle to the progress of negotiations and ultimately to the conference itself. In the preparatory sessions it resulted in uneven progress on issues grouped into three subcommittees. Subcommittees I and III of the Seabed Committee considered the seabed regime and machinery, marine pollution, and scientific research. All other agenda items (such as the territorial sea, economic zone, preferential rights, straits, fisheries, and continental shelf) remained within the purview of Subcommittee II. While the first and third Subcommittees established 33-member working groups, Subcommittee II had one 91-member working group of the whole. Because the agenda items in Subcommittee II touched on the critical issue of the extent of coastal state jurisdiction, no agreement was possible on dividing the issues among smaller working groups. And, given the interdependence of the various agenda items, the work of the other subcommittees on the seabed regime, marine pollution and scientific research was inevitably hindered by delay in the work of Subcommittee II.

The problems of negotiating an international treaty for ocean space did not become easier with the shift from the 91-nation preparatory committee to a 148-member plenipotentiary voting conference. After six years of discussion and preparatory meetings, the Third United Nations Conference on the Law of the Sea opened in New York in December, 1973. The two-week organizing session considered the questions of membership, committee seats, and voting procedures. As agreement could not be reached on the latter, the question of voting procedures was left for the opening weeks of the ten-week Caracas session in the summer of 1974. The Caracas meeting was plagued by the same problems as the preparatory sessions. The progress of the committee handling the sensitive questions of coastal state jurisdiction set the pace for work in the other conference committees. The diversity of state interests in the large number of issues under consideration rendered that progress negligible.

The success or failure of the Caracas and subsequent sessions of the Law of the Sea Conference cannot be found in a treaty adopted by the majority over the strong opposition of the few. Rather, it lies in the creation of institutional mechanisms, whether by a single comprehensive treaty or otherwise, that will be able to accommodate the interests of diverse ocean users in an environment of rapidly changing technology.

73

II. U.S. SECURITY INTERESTS IN OCEAN LAW

ROBERT E. OSGOOD

Dean, The Johns Hopkins School of Advanced International Studies

Director, U.S. Ocean Policy Project

THE NEED FOR REASSESSMENT

In the foreign policy of most nations, security interests are given priority. U.S. ocean policy follows this pattern, but the conception of security underlying this policy has greatly expanded. Since its apparent emphasis on military mobility before the U.S. Draft Seabed Treaty of 1970, security has expanded to include a major concern with unhampered commercial navigation in the period leading to the international law of the sea conference in 1974.

Actually, the appearance that military considerations dominated policymaking in the early period is somewhat misleading. In 1969 and 1970 the formulation of U.S. ocean policy could still be powerfully affected by a forceful individual in a key position in the Department of Defense and complicated political issues were explained and justified in terms of military security needs. At that time the conspicuous role of the Defense Department overshadowed the more fundamental objective of those in the government who were most influential in the formulation of the Draft Seabed Treaty. Their objective was to bring growing competition and potential chronic conflict in ocean space under the control of international law and international institu-

75

tion. Therefore, in the State Department, the National Security Council, and in the Department of Defense (DOD) as well, agreement to an international treaty establishing a narrow continental shelf boundary, international restrictions on the exploitation of ocean resources, a share of revenue from exploitation for economic development, and international regulatory machinery was seen as necessary to America's broadest international interest. By happy coincidence, the narrower interests of DOD corresponded to the larger interest of the United States in preventing an era of international conflict, revolving around competing claims to ocean territory and resources.

As the 1974 international law of the sea conference approached, however, some ocean experts both outside and within the government concluded that this coincidence is no longer so happy. They fear that DOD is locked into an excessively rigid position on free transit through straits—a policy not indispensable to American security but one which may jeopardize the achievement of the kind of minimal international order essential to America's broader ocean interests. The prevailing official position, however, is that the principle of unimpeded passage through straits has become increasingly important because of the growing threat to petroleum and other commercial transit, given the prospect of "subjective" interpretations of innocent passage. Moreover, in international bargaining and negotiating on ocean law, uncompromising U.S. commitment to unimpeded passage is held to strengthen the prospect of achieving a useful, comprehensive, and near-universal law of the sea treaty.

In forecasting the prospect of a law of the sea

treaty, even government experts must rely on reasoned conjecture, while outsiders are at an almost hopeless disadvantage. But an outsider's view of American security interests at stake in ocean law may at least show the full range of these interests and suggest some priorities among them. As in the assessment of most security issues, lack of access to classified data is much less important than one's perspective on the political significance of well-known facts and developments. From this perspective I have undertaken an assessment of U.S. security interests at stake in the developing laws and practices concerning the use of ocean space.[1]

The amount of technical detail involved in assessing the U.S. military security interests in ocean regimes is disproportionate to the relative importance of strictly military considerations. The thesis presented here conforms to the now conventional view that the most important security interests at stake in the law of the sea treaty are more than purely military ones. The policy question involved is whether the official U.S. position may jeopardize the broader interests in attempting to protect the narrower ones or whether, as the top U.S. ocean officials maintain, the law of the sea provisions

[1] In this piece I have relied entirely on unclassified material. Therefore, I cannot vouch for the accuracy of the technical data that does not come from official published sources. Since it would be tedious and cumbersome, I have not cited a source for every piece of data. Aside from the great abundance of such unofficial data in the daily and the technical periodical press, I have relied on a number of special publications, such as the annual *SIPRI Yearbook of World Armaments,* published by the Stockholm International Peace Research Institute; *Jane's Fighting Ships 1973–74* and *Jane's Weapons Systems 1972–73;* and the annual *Military Balance,* published by the International Institute of Strategic Studies.

(particularly, free transit) intended to protect U.S. military interests are indispensable in serving the broader interests (for example petroleum shipping) as well.

U.S. OCEAN SECURITY INTERESTS

In 1970 U.S. security interests in ocean use were articulated largely in terms of naval mobility, and the legal requirements of mobility were formulated largely in terms of "free transit" through international straits. A number of these straits would become territorial waters (permitting only "innocent passage" for American warships) if, as expected, a 12-mile territorial sea boundary were contained in the new international law of the sea treaty that the United States was committed to achieve. More narrow still, the advantage of free transit over innocent passage was defined largely in terms of the maintenance of American strategic nuclear capabilities through the unannounced underwater passage of nuclear-powered submarines carrying nuclear missiles (SSBNs). Less emphasized in public statements were three other security interests:

(a) The limitation of territorial sea boundaries, (which might be expanded from twelve to two hundred miles by virtue of Latin American boundary claims, the assertion of antipollution zones [as by Canada], and the process of "creeping jurisdiction" that would extend the assertion of antipollution and resource-exploitation zones to claims of territorial sovereignty);

(b) The right of military overflight (to which not even innocent passage applies) over key international straits;

(c) The right to emplace antisubmarine listening devices on the continental shelf.

Whatever may be said—on tactical-bureaucratic as well as substantive policy grounds—for the seeming priority of military security interests, subsequent developments in the international environment affecting the law of the sea treaty and American ocean interests have called for a reassessment of U.S. ocean security interests. In a larger framework of security interests, the United States needs to use four zones of ocean space—the seabed, subsurface, surface, and superjacent air—in order to support four kinds of functions that enable the United States to sustain important domestic and foreign interests:

(a) The maintenance of an adequate strategic nuclear capability in relation to the Soviet capability,

(b) The maintenance of an adequate capacity to project American forces overseas in limited wars,[2]

(c) The maintenance of adequate intelligence and military surveillance capabilities,

(d) The protection in peacetime of U.S. citizens, commerce, access to critical resources, and a variety of specific policy objectives overseas.

These functions can be regarded as components of U.S. national security insofar as they support American military security, important external interests, and the welfare of American citizens. This is a broad and rather amorphous definition of security since the objects to be secured go far be-

---

[2] I assume that in a general war the peacetime regimes governing the use of the oceans would be irrelevant, whereas in a war significantly limited geographically and in other respects these regimes might be observed to some extent.

yond the territorial integrity of the United States itself, but it is in accord with the tremendous postwar expansion of the American conception of national security to encompass the security of allies, a wide range of foreign commitments and other concerns, and an international environment congenial to the protection of these interests. To be sure, the nation is moving toward a more limited and selective interpretation of its security interests, particularly insofar as these interests require the use of armed force. But having acquired global commitments as the dominant counterpoise to the rival superpower, the United States is not about to revert to its restricted, pre-World War II concept of national security.

THE FOREIGN POLICY CONTEXT

Assessment of the importance of these various security functions depends first upon the impact of the changing international environment on America's vital foreign interests and on the requirements of maintaining them against possible threats. Enough time has now passed since the announcement of the Nixon Doctrine, the American withdrawal from the Vietnam war, and the rapprochement with China to make some reasonably confident conjectures about the nature of American security policy and its international environment for the next decade.

It is now clear that the foreign policy instituted and consolidated by the Nixon administration seeks to maintain the U.S. position as a superpower with global interests, global political/military commitments, and global influence, but at a moderated level of expense and diminished direct (especially military) involvement. This posture can be described as retrenchment without disengagement.[3] Toward this end the primary foreign concern of the U.S. government is to orchestrate a global *modus vivendi* of interlinked agreements and understandings with the nation that is potentially most dangerous to the United States: the USSR. Diplomatically and politically, it seeks to promote this aim through rapprochement with the People's Republic of China, the normalization and stabilization of relations between the two Germanies, the control of superpower competition in the less developed Third World, and the insulation of détente from the superpowers' involvements in this area. Economically, it seeks to promote this global arrangement through the transfer of capital and agricultural goods to the Soviet Union to sustain a Soviet policy and regime committed to détente. Militarily, the U.S. aims to undergird the global *modus vivendi* with stabilization of the U.S.-Soviet military balance and moderation of the arms competition through mutual acceptance of strategic parity (as in SALT) and with mutually agreed limitations on European forces and opposition to the emergence of new independent national nuclear forces.

The Nixon administration's second concern is to reconstruct its relations with America's major allies—the NATO countries and Japan—so as to give them a compelling interest in participating in the new détente relationships with the Soviet Union and the People's Republic of China on somewhat revised terms: greater diplomatic independence and

[3] See *America and the World,* vol. II: Robert E. Osgood and others, *Retreat from Empire? The First Nixon Administration* (Baltimore: Johns Hopkins University Press, 1973), chap. 1.

initiative, accommodation with the United States of increasingly divergent trade and monetary interests, and increased contribution to collective defense under continuing preponderant American management.

As for the Third World—composed largely of new and poor countries and scarcely five years ago thought to be the decisive arena of the Cold War —the Nixon administration hopes to lower America's profile by leaving the welfare and security of less developed countries primarily to their own individual and collective efforts of self-help. Having reduced the official estimate of the Communist (and particularly the Chinese) threat of military attack and subversion in the Third World and having raised the official estimate of the capacity of weak states to resist Communist control imposed from the outside, the Nixon administration will rely almost entirely upon the selective use of military and economic aid to contain local Communist aggression. While reaffirming its pledge to shield allies and other states vital to American security from direct aggression by nuclear states, it has virtually ruled out a direct combat role for U.S. forces in local wars that are largely insurgent or civil. The reduction of American military personnel by one third, the reduction of general purpose forces in particular, and the substantial withdrawal of American forces from Asia give tangible meaning to this lowering of the American military profile in the Third World.

Judging from official pronouncements, America's military posture supporting the Nixon-Kissinger revision of foreign policy will continue to aim at maintaining strategic parity with the Soviet Union

—indeed, with overall technological equality and a capacity to respond to nuclear attack with something more than massive devastation. The United States will also seek to maintain credible conventional as well as nuclear protection for its allies. But, as compared with the periods after the Korean and during the Vietnam wars, it will be far less (if at all) concerned with maintaining a policy or capacity for waging large-scale local wars, as distinguished from small-scale interventions. And, in any event, its political and material capacity to fight such wars will substantially decline.

The International Political Context

Under what conditions can the United States be expected to retain its position as the predominant manager of the still bipolar, now moderated and stabilized, military balance against the Soviet Union and at the same time retrench its capacity for limited overseas intervention in local wars while maintaining a position of global influence? At the minimum, one must postulate the continuation of U.S.-Soviet détente and of compelling political and military constraints against Communist armed action.

Will these conditions prevail in the coming decade of international politics? Probably so. The past era of intense great-power confrontation and crisis has more than likely ended. A period of great-power diplomatic maneuvering in which superpower crises, military security issues, and concern with the military balance (except in the context of arms control) diminish and recede into the background seems likely to continue for at least a decade. Perhaps this will be a period of considerably less harmonious great-power relations, especially between the United States and its major allies, than the U.S. government anticipates. And perhaps in such a period there will be a greater erosion of the American material capacity and will to maintain a convincing global posture than the Nixon Doctrine presupposes. Eventually, the diffusion of power and interests among the world's five developed centers of power, and the relative decline of American power, could lead to a new, multipolar era of confrontation. But this is too conjectural a possibility to be the basis for changing the American security policy outlined by the Nixon administration.

It is somewhat less conjectural, however, to postulate situations short of large-scale local war in which American security interests may be in jeopardy. Such situations are most likely to arise where indigenous tensions and conflicts threaten (a) the security of friendly regimes and/or (b) the unhindered supply of critical resources, particularly petroleum. In most of these situations the protection of American interests would depend on the local configuration of interests and power. In some cases, however, protection will depend on the use of force and threats of force by indigenous countries, which the United States would support or oppose by arms aid and other indirect means. In rare cases, one can imagine the United States more directly supporting, or threatening to support, friendly regimes against hostile movements and states, especially where such support could be extended by military demonstrations or interpositions incurring a minimal risk of U.S. involvement in war.

Thus in the Jordanian crisis of 1970, the U.S. government evidently contemplated aerial intervention, to rescue hostages seized by Palestinian guerillas and evacuate American civilians, bolster the pro-Western Jordanian regime of King Hussein against the guerillas and Syria, and, above all, to deter the Soviets from taking advantage of the conflict or triggering a larger war. At the same time, the U.S. sought to impress them (and the Arabs) in the wake of the Egyptian missile crisis, with the credibility of American power in the Middle East. Actually, the quick success of the Jordanian army against El Fatah forces and Syrian tanks, combined with Israel's mobilization on the frontier, were decisive in resolving this crisis favorably to American interests. Whether the United States would have intervened under any circumstances must remain in doubt.[4] But the incident illustrates the most likely role of American air, naval, and amphibious forces in a local crisis or war: deterring Soviet direct or indirect intervention; inducing Soviet cooperation toward a peaceful and not unfavorable resolution of the crisis; maintaining Soviet respect for American power in order to prevent the Soviet Union from seeking some regional, unilateral advantage that would jeopardize the network of interlinked constraints in the superpowers' global *modus vivendi*. In addition, the role of American forces might be to rescue or protect American civilians, to support friendly local regimes against hostile states, and to maintain in the eyes of regional states the credibility of American power to protect American interests. The prospect of the United States actually employing its armed forces in local crises and conflicts will remain ambiguous. Nonetheless, military demonstrations, mobilizations, and maneuvers will

[4] On this question, see the somewhat opposing views of Henry Brandon and David Schoenbaum in "Jordan: the Forgotten Crisis," *Foreign Policy* (Spring, 1973), pp. 157–81.

probably be credible enough to be viewed by the American president as an indispensable instrument of policy, lest potential adversaries stumble into a clash of arms by underestimating his will to use force.

In any case, as new and more structured regional patterns of conflict and alignment seem likely to develop in some parts of the Third World, the United States and the Soviet Union can be expected to remain mutually constrained yet interested participants, through military assistance and other means, in the international politics of these regions. They will in some cases, as in the Middle East, be aligned competitively with opposing aspirants to regional hegemony and influence. Where one or both superpowers have important material as well as political interests at stake in regional power politics, they may find themselves backing contenders in local military actions, demonstrations, and even wars in which their own military capabilities will play at least a tacit role.

This trend is growing now in the Persian (or Arabian) Gulf area. Growing dependence on Middle Eastern oil gives the United States a major material stake in an area in which it has had political, commercial, and strategic interests for some time.[5]

[5] In 1973 more than one-third of American oil consumption came from abroad and about 10 percent from the Middle East. Assuming the same rate of increase in U.S. demand, and no imposition of import restrictions, dependence on foreign oil is generally expected to increase to 50 percent of American consumption and dependence on the Middle East to 50 percent of foreign imports in the next five to ten years, before alternative sources of oil and energy could theoretically alleviate this dependence. In 1973, however, only Kuwait and Saudi Arabia had enough foreign exchange reserves to be able to shut down production for a long period.

The increased capacity of a few countries to withhold oil supplies to the United States because of huge currency reserves and alternative buyers, together with the possibility that the Arab-Israeli tension or the influence of radical regimes will provide the political incentive for such withholding, constitutes a new threat to America's regional interests. Similarly, the possibility that local rivalries in the area—resulting, for example, in a conflict between Iraq and Iran, with radical regimes and traditional kingdoms aligning themselves on opposite sides—may disrupt American access to oil poses a potential economic threat with such a serious impact on American domestic welfare as to be tantamount to a security threat.

Whether America's enhanced interest in access to Middle Eastern oil will actually be threatened depends most immediately on the developing pattern of conflict and alignment among the Middle Eastern and particularly the gulf states (which control 60 percent of the world's proved oil reserves),[6]

[6] The most intense rivals in the gulf area are Iran and Iraq. Iran, having undertaken a substantial military buildup with American assistance, has become militarily dominant in the gulf and shows signs of seeking to become an Indian Ocean power. Iraq is engaged in a border dispute with Kuwait. Saudi Arabia, although aligned with neither Iran nor Iraq, and in the long run perhaps a natural opponent of the former, tangibly shares the interest of Iran and the shiekdoms in opposing Soviet-supported South Yemen and the radical contenders for power in Oman and elsewhere. Like Iran, Saudi Arabia receives American military assistance. Pakistan has strengthened its alignment with Iran and has provided military advisors to Abu Dhabi, Kuwait, Muscat, and Oman. India, conscious of its dependence on gulf oil and irritated by Iran's ties with Pakistan, has entered into economic and scientific cooperation with Iraq. This pattern of relations is criss-crossed by territorial disputes and dynastic rivalries among the Arab gulf kingdoms and by rivalry between

on the influence of violent Palestinian groups, on the capacity of radical regimes to gain and expand power, on the policies and actions of other consumer states, and on the vicissitudes of the Arab-Israeli dispute. But the involvement of both superpowers in the politics of the area through their major "clients" and other recipients of support means that there is a possibility of American military demonstration or action to protect access to oil.[7]

Apart from the possibly fanciful scenarios of American military action to protect petroleum supplies, some naval planners and publicists define American security interests as maintaining political influence and pressure in a politically acceptable way through a visible naval presence in areas such as the Gulf and Indian Ocean where the United States cannot afford hostile control of the sea. One need not accept those theories of naval power based on ominous threats to vital lines of commerce and on

---

them and Iran on religious and other grounds. It is linked to the Arab-Israeli dispute by Israel's close relations with Iran, as well as by Israel's material dependence on the United States.

[7] Plausible but unlikely scenarios for such an eventuality might include, for example, an American naval deployment and possible air action to deter Soviet intervention and support friendly regimes against Soviet-supported countries and guerillas in the event of Iranian military action against radical take-overs in the shiekdoms or Saudi Arabia, possibly accompanied by a Saudi appeal for American support against radicals who were threatening to disrupt supply of oil to the United States. American armed intervention against an anti-Israeli closure of production by Saudi Arabia seems less likely except in the context of countering Soviet intervention.

See, for example, Tom Engelhardt, "The New Half-Nelson," *Far Eastern Economic Review,* April 9, 1973, pp. 25 ff., and Cecil Brownlow, "Shift Forced in Military Priorities," *Aviation Week,* February 26, 1973, pp. 3F ff.

overestimates of Soviet power[8] in order to appreciate the significance of a global U.S. naval presence. This significance is enhanced by the facts of increasing U.S. dependence on foreign strategic materials and a declining U.S. presence on foreign land.

The world situations most likely to damage the United States broad security interests in this presumed period of protracted détente, however, may be those which the United States cannot affect by military means, directly or indirectly, and over which it has little or no control by any means. These are situations in which American military mobility, military bases, access to oil, and less tangible security interests are damaged by the hostile actions of the weaker and poorer countries, actions which the U.S. is inhibited from countering by force. At other times these are situations in which the conflicts among other states accidentally impinge on American interests. (This latter type of situation was demonstrated in the "cod war" between Britain and Iceland, which threatened to lead to expulsion of the NATO base from Iceland). If the frustrations and resentments of the less developed countries which are no longer able to exploit Cold War competition should be channeled toward organized harassment and pressure against the developed countries—whether for purposes of revenue, politi-

[8] A balanced assessment of the prospect of crises and conflicts arising from Middle Eastern oil politics and affecting U.S. energy interests appears in Robert E. Hunter, *The Energy "Crises" and U.S. Foreign Policy,* Headline Series, no. 216, June, 1973. On Soviet naval power and policy, see Geoffrey Jukes, *The Ocean in Soviet Naval Policy,* Adelphi Papers, no. 87 (International Institute for Strategic Studies, May, 1972); and Barry M. Blechman, *The Changing Soviet Navy* (Washington: Brookings Institution, 1973).

cal influence, or just nationalist self-assertion—the United States might find its security as threatened as at the height of Cold War competition in the Third World. The rising dependence of the United States and its allies on oil and other natural resources and on straits, seas, and the rights of overflight controlled by developing countries, makes American commercial and military mobility particularly vulnerable.[9] Thus, one of the primary U.S. security imperatives may become the achievement of mutually advantageous and acceptable working relationships with coastal states in the Third World.

Using this line of conjecture, the situations affecting U.S. security are even more hypothetical than during the height of the Cold War. Yet American security policy, for the sake of deterrence or just insurance against serious trouble, cannot prudently be geared only to predictable contingencies. With this in mind, we can explore the implications of these security considerations for U.S. ocean policy.

U.S. STRATEGIC NUCLEAR INTERESTS IN OCEAN LAW

By viewing America's foreign and security policies within the present world situations, we can estimate the effects of different ocean regimes on those U.S. ocean security interests outlined above. To say that the United States would benefit from maximum military mobility in ocean space (or maxi-

[9] The opportunities and incentives for developing countries to threaten U.S. investments, monetary interests, and access to natural resources as levers for political pressure and harassment are examined by Fred Bergsten in "The Threat from the Third World," *Foreign Policy* (Summer, 1973), pp. 102–24.

mum freedom to emplace listening devices on continental shelves or to conduct offshore electronic intelligence operations) and minimum interference with maritime access to vital resources is too sweeping a generality to be translated into laws of the sea in the real world. Ideal objectives must be considered in light of such questions as: (a) how likely, and by what means, are various states to impede achievement of these objectives; (b) how would such impedence affect U.S. interests; (c) to what extent and in what ways would different regimes for use of the oceans affect such impedence; and (d) how feasible and costly is the achievement of more favorable regimes?

First, let us apply these questions to U.S. nuclear strategic interests in the use of the ocean. Here the chief concern is the effectiveness of U.S. SSBNs—currently the Polaris/Poseidon fleet—because (1) the installation of many independently guided warheads on missiles (MIRVs) and improvements in missile accuracy increase the importance of concealing missiles under the ocean and (2) because the case for free transit of international straits has rested on the security requirements of the U.S. underwater fleet. The U.S. government maintains that the invulnerability of SSBNs and hence their indispensable role in an adequate second-strike force depends on their right to pass through international straits submerged and unannounced. Under existing law only innocent passage, which requires surfacing of all submarines, would be legal in straits that fall within territorial boundaries. This distinction is considered very important since under a 12-mile territorial sea boundary perhaps more than a dozen straits of possible strategic significance would be overlapped by foreign territorial waters.[10]

To assess the validity and practical importance of this position, a number of questions must be answered.

1. Which of the world's international straits (there are 121, according to an unofficial chart devised by the Office of the Geographer in the U.S. Department of State) that would be overlapped by territorial waters if 12-mile boundaries were agreed might also be important for the mobility of the U.S. Polaris and Poseidon fleet in reaching specified target areas?

The strategic importance of straits is a matter of opinion but at a reasonable maximum this category would include, according to information provided by the same chart of the Office of the Geographer, a list of 16: Gibraltar, two Middle Eastern straits (Bab el Mandeb and Hormuz), four Southeast Asian straits (Malacca, Lombok, Sunda, and Ombai-Wetar), Western Chosen strait (between South Korea and Japan), five Caribbean straits (Old

[10] According to Article 6 of the 1958 Convention, submarines passing through international straits "are required to navigate on the surface, and to show their flag." But the official U.S. interpretation of innocent passage (in line with the International Court of Justice's report in the 1949 Corfu Channel case that "States in time of peace have a right to send their warships through straits used for international navigation between two parts of the high seas without the previous authorization of a coastal State, provided that the passage is innocent"), does not concede that advance notice of passage through territorial waters is required. Advanced notice of transit through straits, the U.S. holds, would run the risk of leading to coastal-state control of transit. In practice, however, the United States evidently provides advance notice of surface ships but not submarines (except, perhaps, where secret bilateral arrangements have been agreed).

Bahamas Channel, Dominica, Martinique, Saint Lucia Channel, and Saint Vencent Passage), Dover, Bering, and the Kennedy-Robeson Channels.[11]

Nine of these straits, however, are not really essential to America's strategic capability, and some would in any case fall inside the territory of military allies.[12] The five Caribbean straits are not needed for transit to Polaris/Poseidon patrol stations, since the Caribbean is not an essential launching area. They are not even essential for access to the Caribbean, since there are several passages over 24 miles wide (for example, Mona, Windward, Anegada, and Guadeloupe).

Western Chosen, the western half of the strait between Japan and the Korean peninsula, is only 23 miles wide; but Japan, if not South Korea, would presumably permit U.S. strategic warships routinely to pass through this strait to the Sea of Japan.[13] In any event, the eastern half of the strait,

[11] The chart, entitled "World Straits Affected by a 12-Mile Territorial Sea," capitalizes 16 straits as "major." Of these 16 I have substituted Kennedy-Robeson for Juan de Fuca.

[12] One of the more striking manifestations of the military establishment's tendency to leave nothing to chance, once committed to translate military interests into law, is DOD's unwillingness to depend upon allied permission, as opposed to legal right, for passage through straits. But unless the U.S. Navy plans on enforcing free transit against its allies, the codification of free transit in international law would seem to add nothing to U.S. naval mobility in the improbable event that the allies were unwilling to grant submerged passage.

[13] Conceivably, the consultation clause in the Security Treaty with Japan might be interpreted to require special permission for passage of something as conspicuous as a task force—in which case the Japanese government might be reluctant to risk political opposition by granting permission. But it seems unlikely that the present Japanese government would be similarly constrained from granting occasional submerged passage, unless its growing concern over Soviet military passage impelled it to

Tsushima Strait, is 25 miles wide.[14] The real sufferer from any closure of the Korean straits would be Soviet general purpose forces—they would have to travel more than twice as far from Valdivostok to the Senkakus by going the La Perouse route (north of Hokkaido and south of Sakhalin), thereby affecting Indian Ocean operations, China coast patrols, or submarine deployments from Nakhodka.[15]

Bab el Mandeb offers no significant targeting advantage over the eastern Mediterranean (and transit through the French side of the strait would probably be available anyway). If the Soviet antisubmarine warfare (ASW) presence became oppressive there, or if Gibraltar were closed, the Red Sea could be considered an alternative deployment area. But nearly all targets accessible from there are also accessible from the gulf. Those in areas that could not be reached from the gulf (Eastern Europe, the Baltic coast, and the Leningrad area) could be covered from the Atlantic. Passage through Hormuz is probably not necessary now that the shorter-range Polaris A-1 (with a 1,200 nautical-mile range) and A-2 (1,750 nautical miles) have been phased out in favor of the A-3 (2,880 nautical

---

apply equal restrictions to American ships. In that case, however, it would also oppose an international free transit agreement.

[14] According to one interpretation, however, a strait in which 12-mile territorial boundaries come to two miles apart will be considered as falling within territorial waters.

[15] Significantly, the Japanese government, while agreeing with the general principle of free transit, has been reluctant to relinquish control of Soviet military passage through the Straits of Tsushima and Tsugaru (between Hokkaido and Honshu) under the anticipated 12-mile boundary. On the other hand, they may also see some advantage to Soviet military use of the strait, in that this facilitates Japanese surveillance.

miles). With Holy Loch available on the west coast of Scotland, there is no great need for SSBNs to use Dover in the English Channel.

2. In which of the remaining straits is submerged passage physically feasible but politically unobtainable on a reliable basis?

Malacca is too shallow (10–12 fathoms) and too busy for submerged passage. Sunda is barely deep enough (20 fathoms in the approaches) but requires a passage of over 700 miles within a 50-fathom depth. The Bering Straits, although about 45 miles wide, are split by Diomede and Little Diomede Islands, making each half of the straits less than 24 miles wide. But since Little Diomede belongs to the United States, submerged passage to the Arctic is not in question politically. Similarly, the narrow route to the Arctic through the Kennedy-Robeson Channels is presumably accessible by submerged passage, since it is in Canadian waters.

This leaves Gibraltar and two Indonesian straits, Ombai-Wetar and Lombok, as strategically important straits through which the submerged passage of U.S. SSBNs is now physically and politically feasible but which might be politically questionable if a 12-mile territorial boundary were established.

The two Indonesian straits are important to SSBN operations from the Indian Ocean to Guam. Without submerged passage through them, the U.S. would have to circumnavigate Australia (greatly reducing the number of days on active patrol), or double back to one of the entrances to the Timor Sea, 180 to 500 miles east of Ombai-Wetar (which would still pass through Indonesian waters).

An additional hindrance to secret passage through

Indonesian waters is Indonesia's interpretation of the archipelago principle of enclosed waters—the two strategically important straits are claimed to be internal rather than international waters.[16] Although the Indonesian government has argued that the archipelago principle does not infringe on innocent passage, it requires prior notification of transit by foreign warships and has begun to raise questions about the innocence of super-tanker passage because of the danger of pollution. In April, 1972, Chairman of the Joint Chiefs of Staff Admiral Thomas H. Moorer declared, "We should have and must have the freedom to go through, under, and over the Malacca Strait." Shortly thereafter, the chief of staff of the Indonesian navy was reported as warning, "Our armed forces will attack any foreign submarines entering territorial waters without permit, because it means a violation of Indonesia's sovereignty."[17] In spite of Indonesian jurisdictional claims, the United States maintains that the Indonesian straits are international. According to press accounts and Indonesian sources, however, the U.S. routinely provides prior notification of transit by surface ships and presumably (if only as a practical convenience) relies on some special bilateral navy-to-navy arrangement for submerged passage consist-

[16] In December, 1957, the Indonesian government declared that "all waters surrounding, between, and linking the islands belonging to the State of Indonesia . . . constitute natural parts of inland or national waters under the absolute jurisdiction of the State of Indonesia . . . . The 12-miles of territorial waters are measured from the line connecting the promontory point of the islands of the Indonesian state." Embassy of Indonesia, *Report on Indonesia* (Washington, D.C.: November–December, 1957, January, 1958), vol. 8, no. 7.

[17] Captain Edward F. Oliver, "Malacca: Dire Straits," *U.S. Naval Institute Proceedings* (June, 1973), p. 29.

ent with the requirements of concealing the details of SSBN passage from foreign intelligence.[18] Although this *modus vivendi* is rather contingent, it satisfies America's needs as long as an Indonesian government as friendly as that of Suharto is in power.

Gibraltar presents a more complicated situation. Although the strait is only 11.5 miles wide and Spain claims a 6-mile territorial sea, its international character has been preserved by historic tradition and by the treaties of 1904 and 1912 among Britain, France, and Spain to secure free passage. In March, 1971, however, foreign rights of transit became more restrictive when Spain and Morocco agreed to cooperate to "promote the creation of Mediterranean awareness" and to consult on all matters of peace and security in the Mediterranean, particularly in the strait. In June, 1972, the Spanish government announced at the UN that the freezing of naval forces and subsequent progressive reductions in the Mediterranean should be considered. At the same time, it indicated the necessity for some compromise between free transit and the rights of coastal states, such compromise to be achieved by a redefinition of the right of innocent passage.

Thus Spain may have prepared the way for asserting a unilateral right to force submarines passing through the Strait of Gibraltar to surface. On the other hand, the effect of such a claim on U.S. SSBNs will depend primarily on the political relations between the United States and Spain. As long as U.S. submarines are based at Rota, submerged

---

[18] The U.S. government officially denies that it has any agreement with any country to provide advance notice of the passage of warships through international straits.

transit of U.S. submarines will be permitted through the Strait of Gibraltar. However, even the closure of Gibraltar to unannounced submerged U.S. submarine passage would not be disastrous to America's strategic capability. After all, the Polaris/Poseidon system can target the entire Soviet Union from the Atlantic and Pacific Oceans and the Arabian Sea. Although there has apparently been no need for SSBN patrols in the Indian Ocean, an Indian Ocean base—say, Diego Garcia—would obviate the need to use Gibraltar or the Indonesian straits altogether.

3. To what extent would surface transit of U.S. SSBNs through straits impair their invulnerability to Soviet detection, identification, and—in the event of war—destruction?

This question really subsumes several others.

(a) Is it more difficult for the Soviets to detect and identify submerged U.S. SSBNs coming through straits than it is for them to detect surfaced SSBNs?

The answer is surely "yes" (assuming, of course, that submerged transit is not announced in advance to the straits state, thus alerting Soviet intelligence). It is relatively easy to detect surface passage through straits by means of surface vessels, land observers, or satellites. By far the most effective and practicable means of electronic surveillance of submerged vessels is a series of hydrophones (or sonars) connected by undersea cables anchored to the continental shelf, like the U.S. CAESAR and COLOSSUS system. But this device has to be hooked up to a listening station on the shore, which would seem to preclude the Soviet Union installing it at Gibraltar or in Indonesia for the foreseeable future.[19] Moreover, in the high traffic-density straits of Gibraltar and Lombok it would be very difficult to single out transiting nuclear submarines from the high level of background noise. Even in the less-traveled Ombai-Wetar, possible Soviet hydrophone arrays would have to be supplemented by "trawlers" or towed arrays to be effective. The United States and the Soviet Union have developed ocean surveillance satellites, but U.S. efforts to use them to detect submerged vessels have proved impractical for basic physical reasons that technology seems unlikely to overcome in the near future. The Soviets would enhance their submerged detection capability if they were willing to assign nuclear-powered anti-submarine submarines (SSNs) to monitor the critical straits; but the difficulty that Soviet SSNs have had in shadowing U.S. SSBNs from bases indicates that SSNs would be no substitute for fixed hydrophone arrays.

(b) To what extent can the Soviet Union continually locate U.S. SSBNs after passage through straits, assuming that Soviet surveillance detects and identifies these SSBNs?

It is now extremely difficult, and promises to remain so for the indefinite future, to track submarines that have passed submerged through straits.

---

[19] Hydrophone arrays towed by surface ships can be almost as effective as implanted systems, but the cost is much greater. Moreover, it is unlikely that towed arrays could avoid extended territorial seas off straits any better than implanted arrays. It is technically possible to deploy implanted arrays at great distances from shore stations, but the need for amplifiers and the problem of breaks and maintenance make this option unattractive.

It is virtually impossible to track all SSBNs on patrol (that is, in position to fire).[20] Open-area surveillance from aircraft, surface ships, and satellites will remain of limited effectiveness unless and until large parts of the ocean floor are covered with a network of bottom detection systems in communication with surface ships and aircraft. The most effective ASW method in wartime is a forward barrier-control system, utilizing coordinated bottom detection devices, other sensors, attack submarines, and ASW aircraft. In peacetime, however, this system cannot prevent SSBNs from passing through the barrier and disappearing.

(c) Would the Soviet capacity to destroy U.S. SSBNs tracked and located after detected passage through straits significantly affect the U.S. second-strike capability?

This is unlikely, unless one estimates the requirements of an adequate second-strike capability very conservatively. To reduce the U.S. second-strike

---

[20] Thus Secretary of Defense Laird stated in February 20, 1970, "according to our best estimates, we believe that our Polaris and Poseidon submarines at sea can be considered virtually invulnerable today. With a highly concentrated effort, the Soviet Navy might be able to localize and destroy at sea one or two Polaris submarines. But the massive and expensive undertaking that would be required to extend such a capability using currently known techniques would take time and would certainly be evident." He added, however, "A combination of technological developments and the decision by the Soviets to undertake a worldwide ASW effort might result in some increased degree of Polaris/Poseidon vulnerability beyond the mid-1970's. But, as a defense planner, I would never guarantee the invulnerability of *any* strategic system beyond the reasonably foreseeable future, say 5–7 years." Statement before joint session of Senate Armed Services and Appropriations Committee, cited in SIPRI *Yearbook of World Armaments and Disarmament, 1970–71*, p. 122.

capability significantly, the Soviets would have to simultaneously knock out most of the 20 to 25 U.S. SSBNs on station. Merely a few Poseidon-carrying submarines (which will eventually comprise 31 of the 41 U.S. SSBNs), each carrying 16 missiles with 10 MIRVs on each missile, could overwhelm the Soviet ABM system. Moreover, this situation will last at least as long as the initial Strategic Arms Limitation Treaty limiting deployment of ABMs is in effect.

4. How will the prospective new Trident SSBN system affect the need to use the critical straits in question?

Although the amount of congressional funding and the outcome of efforts in the Strategic Arms Limitation Talks to limit SSBNs are uncertain, the development of a new Underwater Long-Range Missile System (ULMS) for the Trident SSBN system may, in the 1980s, produce a successor to Polaris/Poseidon. The Trident submarine would carry 24 missiles with MIRV warheads having a range of between 4,500 and 6,500 nautical miles. It would be quieter, dive deeper, and remain on station for longer periods. Deployment of the Trident system—or deployment of ULMS on Poseidon submarines, planned for fiscal 1978—would virtually obviate the dependence of the U.S. underwater nuclear force on transit of straits.

Given these considerations, a law of the sea treaty sanctioning 12-mile territorial boundaries but excluding free transit of international straits would not seriously weaken nuclear deterrence, although it would make operation of the U.S. SSBN fleet more difficult. From an operational standpoint having to surface would be more difficult for nuclear antisubmarine submarines (SSNs), which play an important role in the strategic nuclear equation. Even though surface transit of SSNs would give Soviet intelligence more information, it would neither increase the willingness of the Soviet Union to launch a nuclear first strike nor greatly enhance the efficacy of Soviet salvos after an initial nuclear exchange. In any event, the same requirements of surfacing imposed on Soviet SSNs would offset the disadvantage to the U.S. underwater deterrent.

Aside from the problem of detection, however, there are other operational disadvantages to surfacing nuclear submarines in straits. Where high-density traffic occurs, as in narrow straits and around headlands, the nuclear submarine is safer both to itself and to surface shipping when it is below the surface. One reason is its huge size. An advanced model such as the *Lafayette* is 425 feet in length, has a beam of 33 feet and a submerged displacement of 8,750 tons, which is longer than World War II destroyers and heavier than some World War II light cruisers. The nuclear submarine is designed to operate best when submerged, where she has greatest maneuverability and her sensors work best. With a low conning tower and very little superstructure, she must waive some construction standards in order to comply with light requirements for night navigation. For this reason, and since much of her hull is below the surface and not visible to electronic searchers (radar), merchantmen find a submarine hard to detect. Moreover, a submarine's ability to travel under the surface frees her from the limitation of surface weather and wave motion, and any submarine is particularly vulnerable to collision because of its small reservoir of bouancy.

The operational disadvantages of surface transit could be avoided, of course, if the United States would give littoral states advance notification of underwater transit, providing that the critical states in question would regard underwater transit on these terms as a satisfactory arrangement. But this hypothesis only illustrates that the prior issue is the importance of secret passage.

When pressed to explain the necessity for free transit of straits, U.S. officials have referred not only to the security of secret passage and to the safety of submerged passage but also to the prospect that, without an international treaty prescribing free transit, straits states might resort to "subjective" (that is, politically inspired) interpretations of innocent passage to restrict the passage of U.S. warships. Thus John R. Stevenson, chief of the U.S. delegation to the UN Seabed Committee, testified before Congress that "We would not contemplate notifying [littoral states of intention to transit straits] because if such a requirement is introduced, there is of course ultimately a risk of this leading to control of transit through straits." This risk, Stevenson said, lies mostly in the future, and he cited no case in which the requirement of advance notification had been used to restrict naval transit.[21]

---

[21] Testimony on April 10, 1973, before the Subcommittee on International Organizations and Movements, House Committee on Foreign Affairs, 92nd cong., 2nd sess., p. 12. Stevenson and Jared Carter, of the Department of Defense, substantiated the risk by citing Egypt's denial of passage to a commercial vessel in the straits leading to the Gulf of Aqaba before the June, 1967, Arab-Israeli war, on the grounds that the cargo

The risk of restrictive interpretations of innocent passage, however, applies largely to commercial vessels on grounds of navigational safety and antipollution. This point has recently received considerable attention, after years of neglect, because of the oil industry's heightened interest in unencumbered shipping. Safety and antipollution would seem to be objectively important grounds for controlling the passage of ships offshore. But let us assume that there is a real danger that littoral states will interpret innocent passage and the requirement of advance notification in order to deny transit of straits to American warships for purely political reasons. Then why would these states sign a treaty prescribing unimpeded passage or be deterred by such a treaty?

Aside from SSBNs, there are other components of the U.S. strategic capability which deserve our attention. In the controversy over free transit through straits, the issue of overflight has been virtually ignored in public statements, although the U.S. position on the law of the sea treaty, presumably for strategic reasons, prescribes free transit over straits for military aircraft. (International law does not recognize innocent passage for overflight.) According to the prevailing official Triad nuclear deterrent system, the U.S. strategic nuclear capability requires manned aircraft as well as SSBNs and land-based missiles. The U.S. strategic bombing force is still a significant weapons system, with some

---

bound to Israel was not innocent. (Egypt, however, based its contention on the position that there had been a state of war since 1948). Carter added that there were other examples of states claiming that warships do not have the right of innocent passage.

distinct advantage of mobility and of control responsive to political guidance. One might suppose that effective denial of military overflight over key straits would seriously impair the utility of the U.S. strategic bombing force as a deterrent. In practice, however, the right to fly over 24-mile straits has not proved critical to the U.S. strategic bomber force (as distinguished from the U.S. military airlift capability). Overflight of straits is only a small part of the pattern of overflight, managed by special arrangements, where necessary, and physically infeasible for most states to deny in any case.[22]

Perhaps a more serious issue involving overflight is the operation of ship-borne aircraft during transit. In the South Pacific and the Caribbean, the use of helicopters during the transit of certain straits by deep-draft vessels is useful for such navigational purposes as screening for opposed exits from the strait. But Indonesia already has protested the operation of helicopters from a Seventh Fleet CVA during passage through the archipelago. COD (Carrier Onboard Delivery) aircraft in the Eastern Indian Ocean or Indonesian waters might come under similar protest unless they went over Thailand,

[22] In those nations where the United States has its own bases or regular access to foreign bases, the United States has interpreted overflight rights to be implicit in permission to use the bases. If there are no such base rights, permission for overflight is supposed to depend on diplomatic clearances (received by filing one-time transit requests with the defense attaches three or four days in advance of the flights). In emergencies the U.S. practice has been to get clearance, go around, or, infrequently, fly over without clearance. In practice, the distribution of American bases has obviated serious overflight restrictions. In the Middle East crisis of November, 1973, however, only Portugal granted the United States overflight, thereby making it necessary to fly over the Strait of Gibraltar.

with which the U.S. has an agreement. The airlift of troops to the Indian Ocean region could be seriously hindered by lack of overflight rights, much as the redeployment of troops to Lebanon was held up for the same reason in 1958.

The emphasis in American ocean policy on free transit under, through, or over international straits has somewhat overshadowed another official concern: that the U.S. strategic capability may be hampered by territorial or continental shelf jurisdictions claimed or established by coastal states.

The breadth of the continental shelf under national jurisdiction might have some effect on the freedom of the United States to place passive ASW listening devices (SOSUS) on the shelf, particularly off the shores of foreign countries.[23] Apparently, these devices are most effective beyond the 200-meter depth and part way down the slope of the

[23] See, particularly, the proceedings of 1969–70 in the Eighteen Nation Disarmament Committee (ENDC), renamed the Conference of the Committee on Disarmament (CCD) in August 1969, which led to the 1971 *Treaty on the Prohibition of the Emplacement of Nuclear Weapons and Other Weapons of Mass Destruction on the Seabed and the Ocean Floor and in the Subsoil Thereof.* Edward Duncan Brown draws principally from these and other UN documents, such as the proceedings of the Seabed Committee, in examining the legal status of passive listening devices on the continental shelf in *Arms Control in Hydrospace: Legal Aspects* (Woodrow Wilson International Center for Scholars, Ocean Series 301, June, 1971), pp. 22–35. See also *SIPRI Yearbook of World Armaments and Disarmament, 1969–70,* pp. 154–79; Captain L. E. Zeni, "Defense Needs in Accommodations Among Ocean Users," in Lewis M. Alexander, ed., *Law of the Sea: International Rules and Organization for the Sea* (Kingston: University of Rhode Island, 1969), p. 33; John A. Knauss, "The Military Role in the Ocean and its Relation to the Law of the Sea," in Lewis M. Alexander, ed., *The Law of the Sea: A New Geneva Conference* (Kingston: University of Rhode Island, 1972).

shelf,[24] although their effectiveness also depends on the peculiar acoustic properties of the ocean at various temperatures, depths, and salinity and particularly on the depth of the sound channel that focuses sound energy in deep water. Presumably, the United States would not place SOSUS on shelf areas restricted by existing international law or protected by a new international treaty. Therefore, if SOSUS is vital to America's strategic capability, any ocean regime that extended territorial sovereignty over the whole continental margin would adversely affect U.S. military security if SOSUS is vital to America's strategic capability.

Whatever the strategic or other military importance of ASW,[25] hydrophone arrays on the

[24] One can infer this from the fact that the original U.S. position on the prospective law of the sea treaty implicitly protected the legal right of the United States to emplace such devices on the continental shelf beyond the 200-meter depth. See also Knauss, "The Military Role in the Ocean," p. 79. Article 3 of the U.S. Draft Seabed Treaty provides that the area beyond this depth "shall be open to use by all States, without discrimination, except as otherwise provided in this Convention." The only exception pertains to the exploration and exploitation of certain natural resources. In tabling the treaty, U.S. representatives, in a studied reference to military uses of the seabed, pointed out that it expressly protected the rights of states to conduct activities other than exploration and exploitation of certain natural resources in the area beyond the 200-meter isobath.

[25] The utility of ASW as a deterrent to a nuclear attack would seem to be negligible since its contribution to the U.S. second-strike capability by protecting SSBNs is insignificant as compared with the other components of this capability. ASW would play a major role, as a part of the U.S. strategic warfighting capability, particularly in protecting convoys. But the utility of protecting convoys in any reasonably imaginable war with the USSR is highly questionable. Moreover, the efficacy of ASW against SSNs is probably declining. For a balanced and skeptical analysis of the role of naval forces in general war, see Laurence W. Martin, *The Sea in Modern Strategy* (London: Institute for Strategic Studies, 1967), chap. 2.

107

ocean bottom are (and will remain for the next five to ten years) critically important to the U.S. ASW capability. These acoustic devices may be vulnerable to Soviet interference, but it is safe to assume that the Soviets are installing many of the same kind of devices and therefore have a vested interest in not interfering with those of the U.S. Most developing countries do not have the capability to locate and destroy the arrays. In any case, the United States denies that it has placed them off their shores.

These facts notwithstanding, the utility of SOSUS would not be critically affected even by the broadest boundary of coastal-state sovereignty on the continental shelf. The crucial monitoring areas where SOSUS needs to be emplaced, one would assume from those submarine passageways where the devices are most useful, are the Greenland-Iceland-United Kingdom gap, the Arctic, the North Pacific, and the Caribbean. With the possible exception of Iceland, enough of the Northern European countries are concerned about the Soviet SSBN force to permit U.S. listening devices in the area. Considering the extent of the shelf off Alaska and Canada, the emplacement of hydrophone arrays in the Arctic is not likely to be severely restricted by a shelf convention. By its possession of Guam, Midway, Hawaii, Alaska, and the Aleutians, the United States owns a significant amount of underwater real estate on which to emplace listening devices in the North Pacific. Whatever gaps may exist in this coverage would not seem to be affected one way or another by extended claims to the continental shelf. Only in the Caribbean and the Gulf of

Mexico would a broad national shelf be likely to restrict U.S. coverage. U.S. coverage in these areas is limited anyway, since Cuba blocks it from the continental U.S. while the Dominican Republic lies in the way of coverage from Puerto Rico.

In any case, as noted above, since hydrophones have to be connected to shore stations (or, at great expense, to surface ships), the United States generally needs the permission of coastal states to emplace SOSUS on their continental shelves, whether within or beyond the territorial boundaries claimed by these states. It should also be noted that an extension of national claims to the shelf edge probably would do more damage to Soviet than to American acoustic installations. It probably would be difficult to find a government beyond the Norwegian Sea that would consent to Soviet devices on its shelf—not to mention objections by Canada and Japan (although the effect of this fact is limited by Soviet ownership of the Kuriles). The implications for SOSUS are the same even if national regimes encompass the continental margin. However, the bottom topography near Iceland makes it difficult to determine the precise limits of the shelf, margin, rise, etc.

There is yet a third possibility if no international regime is agreed upon. The 1958 Continental Shelf Convention states in part that "the term 'continental shelf' is used as referring . . . to the seabed and subsoil of the submarine areas adjacent to the coast to where the depth of the superjacent water admits of exploitation of the natural resources of said areas." Since the technology for exploiting all but the deepest trenches soon will be available, this could eventually lead to a delimitation of the seabed on the basis of median lines. In this event, the United States would own most of the North Pacific seabed (although it probably would not be useful for more listening stations); the United States, Canada, and the USSR would divide the Arctic; the situation in the Caribbean would not be greatly altered; and Norway would own much of the seabed beneath the entrance to the North Atlantic.

Finally, in estimating the impact of alternative ocean regimes on America's military strategic capability, one must take into account the effects of extended territorial sea boundaries and other kinds of offshore zones. These effects, of course, depend in part upon what sort of restrictions coastal states choose to claim and are able to secure by consent or force. Added to the proliferation of extensive off-shore territorial claims, coastal states are looking increasingly to antipollution, security, and other functional zones to restrict foreign navigation, both military and civilian. Moreover, in the absence of a comprehensive and near-universal law of the sea treaty such as the United States has proposed, coastal states may resort to regional or local treaties —on the model of the Montreux Convention or a version of the Soviet doctrine of "closed seas"— that will severely restrict the numbers, types, and transit methods of warships belonging to non-signatories. Assuming, then, for the sake of analysis, that more and more coastal states will be trying to apply more and more restrictions on foreign military passage within 50- to 200-mile off-shore zones and adjacent seas, what are the implications for America's strategic capability?

If one were to select a 200-mile region to impede American naval passage and have the greatest effect on America's strategic capability, it would be Arctic, given the premise presented here that the Mediterranean is not indispensable to America's strategic nuclear capability. But even with 200-mile sea boundaries, access to the Arctic would be possible through the Eastern Bering Strait and the Kennedy-Robeson Channels (given Canadian compliance). In the Atlantic, patrols could still go far north within the 200-mile boundary around the Shetlands. In Indonesian waters, a 200-mile boundary would not be much more restrictive than a 12-mile boundary, since Indonesia defines its boundary according to a broad archipelago doctrine. In any case, Poseidon missiles could still target all the USSR from points 200 miles off Bangladesh and Japan and in the southern Norwegian Sea.

More important than the impact of restrictive territorial zones and special seas on SSBNs may be their impact on the integrated operation of fleets—such as the Sixth Fleet in the Mediterranean—which have strategic functions beyond providing launching platforms for missiles. It should be noted, however, that the strategic function of surface ships, apart from their political and psychological uses, has been drastically eroded by technological advances in attack submarines, surface ships, and aircraft.

Moreover, it is worth noting that coastal state restrictions would have a much more adverse impact on Soviet than on American strategic mobility. If, for example, the restrictions applied to the current narrow sea boundaries were applied to 200-mile boundaries, Soviet SSBNs would be restricted to half of the Arctic and to operations from Petropavlovsk. Submerged passage to the Atlantic would be prohibited. The Caribbean and the southern exits from the Sea of Japan would be closed. Soviet fleet maneuvers would be correspondingly more impeded than American by the proliferation of extensive restricted seas, antipollution zones, and the like.

What, then, are the implications of all these considerations for the protection of American strategic interests under alternative ocean regimes? Unquestionably, America's strategic capability with respect to the Soviet Union would be better off under an effective, universally applicable law of the sea treaty that provided free transit through international straits, established a narrow continental shelf boundary, limited territorial sea boundaries to 12 miles, and protected military passage through antipollution and other zones, than under the more restrictive regimes we have postulated. But even the *most* restrictive of these regimes would not undermine America's strategic capability on the ocean, particularly if the Trident system were in operation. Moreover, the adverse impact of restrictive regimes on Soviet ocean-based strategic capabilities would be far more severe than on American capabilities, although, with America's greater strategic dependence on the sea, her naval leaders cannot be expected to gain much consolation from this comparison.

There is still the question of the most realistic alternative to the postulated proliferation of restrictive regimes. Is it to insist on free transit through international straits and the maximum freedom of the seas against coastal state restrictions? Or is it to concede to coastal states somewhat more extensive control of straits, sea bottoms, and sea boundaries, while protecting the really essential strategic needs, whether through a universal law of the sea treaty or through other kinds of arrangements and agreements?

We shall return to this question after considering America's nonstrategic security needs on the ocean. We should note here that the United States' achievement of special arrangements and agreements that will protect her essential strategic interests—demonstrated in U.S. relations not only with major allies but also with Spain, Indonesia, and Iran—depends on the government's ability to reach favorable bargains in its political relations with key coastal states. In this sense the United States, even in this period of dependence on Middle East oil, has considerable political, economic, and military assets which are seen in its good working relations with a number of locally and regionally powerful states. If this is a correct assessment, it would be a great mistake for the United States to waste political assets or jeopardize other ocean interests in order to achieve maximum strategic advantages in a law of the sea treaty —particularly if pursuit of free transit as a nonnegotiable aim proved unacceptable to key states anyway.

Until recently the heavy emphasis on protection of U.S. strategic nuclear capability has led American ocean law officials, in public statements, to underrate more serious threats to the nation's security interests —many of which impinge on the U.S. capability to conduct limited military actions and demonstrations and to protect vital commerce and other peacetime interests. These same officials also used to underrate America's general security interests, as one of the principal maritime powers, in maintaining harmonious working relations with the less developed coastal states of the world.

We have contended that American security interests will continue to require the support of American armed forces, particularly outside the developed centers of the world and most likely in the Mediterranean–Gulf–Indian Ocean waters providing access to the Middle East. In general terms the revised American foreign policy outlined by the Nixon administration requires maintaining a reduced but still global force for an indefinite period in which moderated great-power competition will be punctuated by continual disturbances on the peripheries of the developed world. This kind of force posture requires great military mobility in ocean space, but the question is how would alternative ocean regimes affect this mobility. American deployment of naval and air forces in ocean space would probably not depend upon territorial sea boundaries of coastal states or on the national positions and international rules governing passage through or over international straits, if the conflict were regarded as sufficiently important to engage American armed forces. Similarly, if America's merchant fleet were to be directly harassed by Soviet or other ships— an unlikely contingency in the case of the Soviet Union, considering its parallel interests as a maritime power—or by denial of access to resources and commerce, the United States would take the measures necessary to protect its vital interests.

Nonetheless, the political nature of some local conflicts might force the United States to honor nonbelligerent states' objections to the passage of U.S. warships and aircraft into their territorial seaspace, especially if the outcome of the conflicts were not critical to American security interests. Thus if the United States were providing material support to a belligerent in a local conflict, either a belligerent's or nonbelligerent's denial of American rights to overflight (as in the Middle East crisis of 1973) or passage of warships and merchant ships would be honored.

In nonmilitary incidents, such as those arising from quasi-legal restrictions imposed on U.S. sea lanes providing access to oil, such denials would be politically difficult for the United States to ignore. In these types of situations, restrictive territorial sea boundaries and special zones can be expected to exert their major impact on America's strategic capability. Thus any imposition by littoral states of restriction on straits is apt to be a far more important and less easily surmounted obstacle to naval mobility (i.e., the transportation of general purpose forces in a crisis) and to the shipping of oil and other resources than to America's underwater strategic nuclear force. Should U.S. security interests require passage through straits of major economic significance, about half (or five) of these could be controlled by states that might impose costly, inconvenient, and, conceivably, politically-inspired restrictions on the passage of goods and resources of value to the United States.[26]

Just such a situation occurred in the Strait of Malacca a few years ago. Concerned about the ecological disaster that could follow an accident to

[26] The following straits could be included in the category of major economic significance (those in italics might be adversely controlled): Florida, Dover, Skagerrak, Bosporus-Dardanelles, Mozambique, *Gibraltar, Hormuz, Bab el Mandeb* (if the Suez Canal were opened), *Malacca, Lombok, Luzon.*

supertankers in the hazardous channels of this strait, Malaysia in July, 1969, claimed a territorial sea of 12 miles. Indonesia, which in 1957 had proclaimed its archipelago doctrine of sovereignty encompassing its 13,000 islands, joined Malaysia in 1970 in a treaty dividing the Strait down the middle. When the carrier U.S.S. *Enterprise* and accompanying ships passed through the strait en route to the Bay of Bengal during the Bangladesh crisis of 1972, Indonesian spokesmen reaffirmed the right of the littoral states to control such passage but reconciled this right with the American action by stating that the Commander of the Seventh Fleet had given advance notice.[27] The United States thus avoided one dispute, but the prospect of more troublesome encounters had been foreshadowed.

It does not necessarily follow, however, that the protection of American interests against such encounters can be secured by new international legal and organizational devices. After the *Enterprise* incident the United States government proposed that a provision for "free passage" of straits in a law of the sea treaty be qualified by international standards for safety which would be established by the Inter-Governmental Maritime Consultative Organization (IMCO) or some other international organization and enforced, beyond the coastal state's territorial sea boundary, by the flag state or port state.[28] But Malaysia and Indonesia, while

[27] Captain Edward F. Oliver, "Malacca: Dire Straits," *U.S. Naval Institute Proceedings* (June, 1973), pp. 27–33.

[28] Within an undefined Coastal Seabed Economic Area, the U.S. position would give coastal states complete authority to enforce both its own and international standards against pollution from seabed activities. With respect to vessels, however, the flag state would continue to have enforcement re-

willing to grant controlled transit through straits and waters near their shores at their discretion (although the United States evidently does not give either Malaysia or Singapore the advance notification Indonesia claims to receive), are not willing to relinquish such control to an international organization dominated by the United States. They are even less willing to entrust enforcement of pollution and safety standards to the great maritime states which continue to congest straits with huge tankers and other commercial vessels.

These political facts favor the adoption of a legal position more accommodating to the claimed residual sovereignty of coastal states beyond their territorial sea boundaries. But it will take more than an international law of the sea treaty to avoid serious conflicts between coastal and maritime states. For example, there now seems to be a *modus vivendi* between the United States and Indonesia that works fairly well although (and perhaps because) jurisdictional differences are not formally resolved. Judging from this case, basic political factors, such as Indonesia's determination to become the dominant Southeast Asian power, its uneasiness about expanding Soviet naval activity and Soviet alignment with India, its latent fear of Japan and reluctance to become dependent on Japan's naval power, and its dependence on an American presence in Southeast Asia, together with American economic assistance and military sales, will have more of an

---

sponsibility beyond the coastal state's territorial boundary, subject to the right of other states to resort to compulsory dispute settlement. The port state could enforce pollution control standards against vessels using its ports, regardless of where violations occurred.

effect on U.S. and Indonesian ocean interests than any law of the sea treaty.

Similarly, the protection of American naval and economic interests in the Persian (or Arabian) Gulf seem far more dependent on good relations with Iran than on a new law of the sea treaty. Indeed, Iran's drive for control of shipping in the gulf, through which two-thirds of the non-Communist world's oil imports pass, tends to conflict with the U.S. proposal for free navigation. Thus in March, 1973, Iran was reported to be exploring an agreement with Oman to inspect all ships passing through the Straits of Hormuz at the entrance of the gulf.[29] Observers of gulf politics regard Iran's announced concern about the threat of pollution as secondary to its concern about other Arab governments supplying arms to Iranian rebels. Iran's inclination to seek control of shipping in the gulf may run counter to an ideal law of the sea treaty, but, considering the more than $2 billion in arms the United States has provided Iran to bolster its supremacy in the gulf, Iran's policy is consistent with American security interests in the gulf. Indeed, if the U.S. does rely on Iran as a surrogate for U.S. naval power in the area, Iranian control of the gulf may be the condition of protecting American interests in the gulf.

Restrictions on overflight in the gulf and Mediterranean regions have a more serious effect on the mobility of general purpose forces in limited wars and crises than on the U.S. strategic capability. In these areas the United States evidently is denied military

[29] *Washington Post,* March 23, 1973, p. A1. Iran and Oman later denied the report. Iran subsequently announced that it was preparing a bill that would extend antipollution controls to 50 miles from shore or the limit of the continental shelf.

overflight rights even by allied and other countries in which it has air bases. As in the case of surface navigation, this enhances the importance of unimpeded passage over straits. In practice, however, the problem of securing essential mobility by overflight is even more confined geographically—essentially the Strait of Gibraltar. In any case, resolving this problem will depend primarily on the political relations with a few key states. If they do not favor unimpeded passage, the key states are not likely to sign a free transit provision because of bargaining at a law of the sea treaty conference. If they do favor passage, the United States might have a better chance of arranging a satisfactory *modus vivendi* outside an international conference than through either a multilateral or bilateral treaty.

Nevertheless, U.S. ocean policy makers still face the troublesome prospect of protecting American ocean security interests through *ad hoc* deals with local and regional powers. They seek to base the protection of American ocean interests on treaty-made laws that apply as generally and unambiguously as possible rather than on less binding arrangements based on fragile political alignments and customary law. Moreover, they look upon both the threat to American ocean interests and the solution to the threat in abstract terms—a practice consistent with the American tendency to identify national interests with a universal order. According to this outlook, the more coastal countries that assert control over straits, claim 50- or 200-mile territorial boundaries, demand special restrictions on innocent passage, or otherwise constrain the use of ocean space, the more likely it is that these nations will clash with the major maritime states. Consequently,

American security interests will face greater danger and the United States will have growing difficulties in moving air and naval units to the sites of crises that affect these interests. Bearing this in mind, government officials believe that without a new universal law of the sea treaty the United States must either acquiesce to claims by coastal states of jurisdictional rights that constrict American ocean mobility or forcefully contest such assertions.

The idea of resorting to force is used to point up the urgency of an international law of the sea treaty, as though force—at least when imposed by the strong against the weak—were either obsolete or too terrible to contemplate. But the generalization is overdrawn. The great powers' constraint in enforcing their interests against the less developed countries depends on a calculus of material (and, one can argue, long-run political) gain and political loss that may change with changing conditions.

Thus, the political costs of the United States forcibly protecting American tuna fishers against the claims of sovereignty by Peru have always seemed excessive compared to what could be gained by such drastic measures and what would be lost without them. It is misleading, however, to infer from this situation that the United States would be equally passive in the face of some threat to a more serious economic interest or to a military security interest. Likewise, British resistance to Iceland's 50-mile exclusive fishing zone claim, which led to a number of clashes between Icelandic naval ships and British escorts, demonstrates considerable British self-restraint but also shows—despite Britain's withdrawal of its warship in pursuit of a settlement—that a maritime state will not necessarily passively accept the assertions by a small state of a conflicting ocean regime when important economic interests are at stake and cannot be secured by other means.

Where military security, rather than fishing rights, is involved, the maritime states have been bolder in backing their interests. The most frequent examples of this have occurred in intelligence gathering. Despite North Vietnam's claim to a 12-mile boundary, the United States acknowledged that the U.S. destroyer *Maddox* was only 11 miles off North Vietnam shortly before the first Gulf of Tonkin incident. In other cases the United States has not been reluctant to fly aerial intelligence missions that contravene jurisdictional claims over coastal-state waters.

In the past decade there have been several cases (excluding fishing-rights interventions and Cold War crises) in which maritime powers have exercised their naval superiority to support their definition of freedom of the seas. In July, 1951, when an Egyptian Corvette intercepted and damaged a British merchantman in the Gulf of Aqaba during an attempted blockade of Israel, a British destroyer flotilla was deployed to the Red Sea. Two weeks later Britain and Egypt reached an agreement on procedures for British shipping in the Gulf. In February, 1957, American destroyers patrolled the Straits of Tiran and the Gulf of Aqaba to prevent Egyptian interference with American merchant shipping en route to Israel. On December 13, 1957, President Sukarno's government enunciated Indonesia's archipelago doctrine. Less than a month later, Destroyer Division 31 passed through the Lombok and Makassar Straits to reaffirm the U.S. right of innocent passage. On July 21, 1961, following a bombardment by French naval aircraft, a French cruiser-destroyer group forced the entrance to the Lake of Bizerta, thereby lifting a Tunisian blockade of the naval base and reestablishing French control. Following Egyptian closing of the Straits of Tiran in May, 1967, the U.S. Sixth Fleet concentrated in the Eastern Mediterranean while the British admiralty announced that the carrier H.M.S. *Victorious* and other units were being kept in the Mediterranean "in readiness against any eventuality," although the threat was not carried further. On April 22, 1969, Iranian warships escorted an Iranian merchant ship from Khorrasmshahr (at the junction of the Tigris and Karun rivers just inside the Iranian border) to the Persian Gulf in defiance of Iraqi threats. Apparently a similar incident had occurred in 1961, but one in which Iran was forced to yield for lack of naval forces.

On other occasions maritime powers simply ignore or reject coastal state claims against their activities. The People's Republic of China routinely challenges U.S. vessels in the Lema Channel en route to Hong Kong, and the U.S. vessels routinely disregard these challenges. Despite protests from other nations, France enforces restricted zones around its nuclear testing site at Mururoa atoll. During the Algerian War, she undertook visit and search of the flagships of more than a dozen nations, on some occasions as far away as the English channel.

Thus, if the jurisdictional claims of coastal states jeopardized American economic or security interests in the Third World, the United States would not necessarily be deterred by immediate political costs from supporting its ocean interests with force.

This would be true especially if the clash occurred out of the context of U.S.-Soviet competition, something increasingly likely to be the case. If such clashes were to become regular features of the international environment, one can even imagine some of the maritime powers at least tacitly cooperating to enforce their conception of freedom of navigation. New laws of the sea would eventually result from the kind of military and diplomatic process, punctuated by test encounters, that created the traditional laws.

It is neither desirable nor necessary, however, that the new laws of the sea would be made in this way. Coastal states and maritime powers have important common interests in preserving the flow of commerce, and neither group is united in opposition to the other. Nevertheless, the prospect of armed encounters may moderate the process of resolving conflicts of national interests. Short of armed force, the protection of American security interests in the ocean will depend on four factors: (1) the configuration of political interests and military power among states in a position to affect vital American military and resource interests; (2) the balance of U.S.-Soviet interests and influence as it affects the actions of these states; (3) the perceived and actual disposition of the United States to back its ocean interests with force and only in this total context; (4) the process of asserting, contesting, accommodating, and negotiating the modalities of the rights of navigation through and over offshore waters and international straits.

With or without a satisfactory law of the sea treaty, the United States, in keeping with the revised view of American power and interests underlying the Nixon doctrine, must depend more and more on the favorable configuration of interests and power among local states rather than on direct American intervention to protect its security interests in the use of ocean space. Insofar as the United States can affect such configurations at all, it must depend primarily on skill and tact in playing the politics of trade and investment, economic and military assistance, and on traditional diplomacy in its dealings with the major oil-producing states and the states astride commercially and militarily key straits.

IMPLICATIONS FOR THE LAW OF THE SEA TREATY

From the standpoint of American security interests, will the projected law of the sea treaty, as discussed here, provide an adequate solution to the various jurisdictional issues concerning the use of the ocean? American law of the sea officials believe that the adoption of a comprehensive treaty, resolving all the issues of military as well as nonmilitary use, would have several advantages over the present system of relying on existing law, separating navigational from other issues for settlement, or on seeking bilateral or regional treaties and arrangements.

One such advantage is *uniformity*. American ocean officials feel that it would be excessively time-consuming, inconvenient, and disorderly to make differing *ad hoc* arrangements with all the littoral states involved. This point is compelling as it applies to jurisdictional zones and other ocean issues affecting commercial activities—whether fishing, petroleum and mineral exploration and exploitation, or merchant shipping. Having to adapt these activities to a diversity of local claims, regulations, and laws could impede commerce, while leaving unresolved many sources of international litigation and conflict. If, for example, littoral states continue to impose an increasing number of more stringent requirements on the type and construction of merchant ships, on insurance, and on navigational taxes and tolls for shipping, the result would be a chaos of claims and arrangements.

This kind of disadvantage, however, is not nearly so serious as it applies to naval and air navigation for security purposes, since the critical problems of military use are not so numerous or diverse as to be beyond satisfactory resolution on an *ad hoc* basis, if necessary.

Of course, as U.S. representatives now emphasize, if a universal law of the sea treaty incorporating free transit could be obtained, it would benefit not only American military mobility but also merchant shipping, in which national commercial and security interests now merge. There would still be a need, however, for special international agreements applicable to merchant shipping. Hence, the U.S. government has (a) stressed that the "free" in "free transit" applies only to unrestricted passage through international straits rather than to all activities on the high seas and (b) expressly stated that the problems of navigational safety and pollution risks in international straits should be resolved by separate international agreements and organizations.[30] If the right of transit must be qualified by

[30] See the statement of John R. Stevenson to Subcommittee II of the UN Seabed Committee, July 28, 1972, UN Doc. A/AC.138/SC.II/SR. 37 at 2; and to the Subcommittee on International Organizations and Movements, U.S., Congress, House, Committee on Foreign Affairs, "Law of the Sea and Peaceful Uses of the Seabeds," 92nd cong., 2nd sess., April 10 and 11, 1972, p. 12.

recognition of the legitimate concerns of littoral states about the hazards of merchant shipping off their shores and in adjacent straits, it may be unwise to combine the protection of this right with the right of submarines to go through straits submerged and unannounced. It may also be unwise to insist on the strict meaning of "free transit" if the substance of the right can be as readily protected in practice—and with less arousal of the political sensitivities of post-colonial states—under the rubric of "innocent" or "unimpeded."

A second ostensible advantage to the comprehensive treaty approach to ocean law-making is that the United States would gain a *bargaining* advantage by combining the free-transit straits provision with resource provisions, such as 200-mile resource zones and revenue sharing. The latter would give coastal states otherwise opposed or indifferent to free transit an incentive to make concessions to U.S. security interests. The only trouble with this argument is that, in practice, the strategy may not work. Indeed, the opposite may occur if coastal states, observing the great importance that the United States attaches to free transit, calculate that they can extract concessions on their control of resource zones and the like as the price of accommodating maritime interests. Judging from the concessions to coastal-state control of resource zones that the United States has already made, the advantage seems to lie with the coastal states. Even where these states (as in Latin America) have evidently made concessions to the U.S. position on free navigation, they have done so in accordance with the Latin doctrine of "patrimonial seas"[31] at the price of American abandonment of opposition to exclusive resource zones.

A third reason for seeking a comprehensive law of the sea treaty is the alleged *political advantage* to negotiating the resolution of conflicting interests in a treaty applicable to *all* states. One supposition underlying this point seems to be that weaker states will find a general multilateral agreement less damaging to their national pride than bilateral or regional arrangements with the United States. The smaller states can explain their accommodations as concessions to the general international community. The United States can avoid the stigma of hegemony and limit the price for compliance the smaller states may exact.

A related supposition may be that in trying to reach bilateral or regional deals the United States must suffer the political embarrassment and the tactical disadvantage of having to satisfy the special interests of weaker states. However, if the United States can generalize its positions and its modes of influence in the United Nations, it will be less vulnerable to such pressure for concessions, and concessions made to one country or regional grouping are less apt to embarrass the United States in dealing with others.

These kinds of political considerations are, of course, valid in some cases of diplomacy; but since they are not always valid only an exploration of the comprehensive law of the sea treaty approach and its alternatives could indicate whether it applies to

[31] A 200-mile area of coastal-state jurisdiction and supervision over the exploration and exploitation of natural resources.

the diplomacy intended to protect U.S. ocean security interests. Here the evidence is likely to remain quite incomplete. Although a number of key coastal states—Spain and Indonesia included—have not yet conceded free transit in return for international controls against accidents and pollution, the United States has nevertheless managed to protect its essential security interests. There is no reason to think that the U.S. would come any closer to gaining acceptance of its position through bilateral or regional deals.

Therefore, it would seem that the case for including the provisions of special security concern in a law of the sea treaty depends not so much on the alleged advantage of comprehensiveness and universality as on the feasibility of persuading a large number of states, including the key straits states, to accept particular provisions like free transit as consistent with their basic interests and sovereignty. If these states agree to free transit, it will not be because of any advantages of political accommodation and bargaining power inherent in the negotiating forum but because of the particular balance of interests that emerges in the total context of their relations with the United States and other maritime states. If they regard free transit as inconsistent with their interests, the United States should not make free transit the condition for accepting a treaty to resolve jurisdictional issues in merchant shipping and commercial activity. American security interests will suffer far more if unresolved jurisdictional issues concerning resource and antipollution zones engender chronic conflicts, and coastal states impose regulations and restrictions on commercial shipping, than if no additional formal agreements on straits were made at all.

As the Third United Nations conference on the law of the sea convened at Caracas, American representatives stoutly insisted that in the end, when a treaty is up for final negotiation, the coastal states will generally accept free transit as compatible with their national interests, and a few countries with maritime interests will see it as a positive advantage. Although there are many skeptics, this estimate may turn out to be correct if the United States makes enough concessions to the pride and interests of enough developing countries. If official optimism about free transit is unwarranted, however, or if the price is exorbitant, the U.S. could best serve her security and ocean interests by confining the law of the sea treaty's international straits passage provisions to general principles of mutual maritime- and coastal-state interest, leaving the precise conditions of transit legally ambiguous. If these conditions need to be made more precise, the United States can delay their formulation until the United States and the key straits states reach an accommodation *outside* an international conference. Indeed, this may be the only course it *can* afford. In any event, the best alternative to protecting U.S. security interests in a comprehensive international treaty is probably not seeking protection through bilateral or regional treaties but simply through informal arrangements under existing law, leavened by international agreements that littoral states, along with the great maritime users, should have a fair share of control over the increasingly congested commercial ocean lanes.

129

The weakness of this alternative has been exaggerated by the official assumption that there is some great advantage to getting many countries to sign an international treaty embodying free transit, although the key straits states refuse to sign it (which U.S. ocean officials concede is likely). The most important objective of a treaty provision on free transit is to gain full legal recognition of the principle of unimpeded passage through straits from the few states that might impede passage—for military purposes, perhaps only Spain and Indonesia. It is unlikely that the U.S. position would be based on the supposition that the key straits states will subordinate their special interests to "world opinion." Therefore, the government must assume that, in the event of a show-down, the United States will be in a better position physically to resist assertions of control by these states, forcibly if necessary, if it can bolster its resistance with the sanction of a nearly universal treaty. There may be an element of truth in this calculation in so far as it applies to the moral courage of American statesmen; but it does seem naive to think that even a multitude of signatures to an international treaty would in itself induce the key opponents of free transit to sign or to comply with a provision they refused to sign.

The assumption of an international treaty's favorable effect on the behavior of reluctant states would be more convincing if there were more reason to share the official U.S. confidence in the eventual "rationality" of a large bloc of coastal and less developed countries that now oppose a free transit provision. Against this hopeful prospect one must weigh the danger that the United States will only aggravate the problem of reconciling its interests in unencumbered navigation with the interests and pride of a large number of coastal states in controlling the use of "their" waters by insisting on the maximum guarantees for its interests through international law. By elevating a set of political accommodations between the interests of the great maritime states and many coastal states into a matter of legal rights and national sovereignty, the United States may only polarize the issues. On the other hand, by asking for less in law, it may get more protection for its interests in fact. For on the practical basis of day-to-day dealings most coastal states, including the key ones, are not necessarily opposed to granting in practice what they may refuse to accept as a legal principle. And if the less developed coastal states do not see themselves and the great maritime states in a contest of power (a contest in which they must rely on their superior voting strength in the UN), many of these states whose shipping can be hampered by regional rivals may conclude that they have as much interest as the developed states in unencumbered navigation.

In this "era of negotiation" and of American "retrenchment without disengagement" it behooves the United States to deal with all states—but particularly with the sensitive less developed states of the Third World, who are undergoing a much-needed redefinition of their interests—on terms of practical mutual benefit and respect, as free as possible from ideological and nationalistic preoccupations. There are critical limits to which the United States can insist upon codifying into international law the protection of interests of a few great maritime states without jeopardizing both the legal progress and the political accommodations upon which it rests.

Library of Congress Cataloging in Publication Data

Hollick, Ann L
    New era of ocean politics.

    (Studies in international affairs, no. 22)
    Includes bibliographical references.
    1. Ocean bottom (Maritime law) 2. Marine resources
and state. 3. Territorial waters. I. Osgood, Robert
Endicott. II. Title. III. Series: Washington
Center of Foreign Policy Research. Studies in inter-
national affairs, no. 22.
JX4426.H64   341.44'8   74–6833
ISBN 0–8018–1633–5
ISBN 0–8018–1634–3 (pbk.)